The Mar

Movement

&

A Brief History of (Some) U.S. Social

Movements

~ 1830s to 2015 ~

Nadine Rosechild Sullivan, Ph.D.

The Marriage Equality Movement

© 2015 Nadine Rosechild Sullivan, Ph.D.

Lifting Consciousness Press

Philadelphia

Table of Contents

INTRODUCTION...5

ORIGINS OF SOCIAL MOVEMENTS.....................................11

ORGANIZATION 13

REPERTOIRE 14

MOVEMENTS WITHIN MOVEMENTS 14

Liberal/Radical 14

Political/Cultural 16

U.S. SOCIAL MOVEMENTS...18

HISTORICAL DEVELOPMENTS 18

ABOLITION 20

LABOR..21

PROGRESSIVE REFORM MOVEMENTS 24

FIRST-WAVE WOMEN'S RIGHTS ACTIVISM....................25

AFRICAN AMERICAN MOVEMENTS 28

NEW LEFT...44

PEACE/ANTI-WAR MOVEMENTS 45

SECOND-WAVE WOMEN'S RIGHTS ACTIVISM 48

FREE LOVE AND BEYOND: SEXUAL FREEDOM MOVEMENTS 53

U.S. LESBIAN AND GAY MOVEMENTS................................55

Homophile Movement 58

Resistance & Pride..61

Gay Social Movement Organizations...................................62

Sexual Liberation 65

Anti-Gay Backlash..65

Plague...66

Cultural/Coming Out Movement 69

3

THE MARRIAGE EQUALITY MOVEMENT..73

  Background – The Demand & The Debate...73

  Defining Marriage - Origins...77

  Ancient and Feudal Economics...78

  Arranged Unions..79

  From Secular to Religious...80

  The "Collapse" of "Traditional" Marriage...81

  Evidence of Same-Sex History...83

  Modern Same-Sex Relationships..86

  The Marriage Equality Movement..88

CONCLUSION 93

BIBLIOGRAPHY 100

ENDNOTES...122

Introduction

When we look through the lens of social movements, the best, and the worst, in human nature is made visible. The ongoing social justice project of conceptualizing and demanding *"liberty and justice"* for *"all,"* has inspired heroism and cooperation that reveals the sublime and the compassionate within us, even as the oppression that necessitates them, and the backlash they draw, reveals the unwashed underbelly of ignorance and hate. When the oppressed (and their allies) confront Power, when those who are mistreated stand up for their collective selves, we find ourselves rooting for the underdog and envisioning the change that may be possible in our own lives. Like great art, majestic music, or sweeping architecture – from the stirring manifesto to the courageous display of civil disobedience and resistance – the public spectacle of liberation unfolds, lifting our eyes to the heights, and allowing us to dream.

In a more practical sense, in the United States, an ideology of government that is (or can, or should, be) *"by the people, for the people,"* is created in the outworking of the belief that *"governments derive their just powers from the consent of the governed,"* and that it is the *"right of the People to alter"* their government into one to which they can consent, through the exercise of their rights to *"freedom of speech,"* freedom *"of the press,"* *"peaceable . . . assembly,"* and *"petition"* for *"a redress of grievances."*[1]

Movements contribute to *social justice* – by demanding that governments be, both, honest and the guardians of citizens' rights – by demanding that governments force dominant groups to share the pie with groups that have been subordinated. Movements allow disenfranchised groups to press for their own inclusion *as enfranchised* (literally and figuratively). Little by little, they break down the barriers of social stratification and entrenched *dis*-privilege – racism, nativism, sexism, heterosexism, cissexism, classism, militarism, ableism, ageism, and more.

Through the study of social movements, we grow to appreciate the price paid for the still-flawed degree of inclusivity we have today; and through the transmission of social movement narratives, we raise up future generations vigilant to protect these hard-won enfranchisements.

Social movements do not so much ask the privileged to lose their privilege.

They do not demand that the hitherto privileged be unjustly immiserated[2] or disenfranchised. The purpose of social justice is NOT served if the privileged become mistreated and oppressed in their stead.

They ask *not* that the privileged leave the table of abundance, only that they allow the dis-privileged Other a seat at the table as well.

They *do* demand that the privileged stop perpetrating *dis*-privilege.

They ask that the historically disenfranchised be also enfranchised, and then, have their enfranchisement codified, enshrined, and guarded in perpetuity.

They expect that the real gut-and-core, fought-for, freedoms of those who face down *prejudice, discrimination, mobs, cavalry, national guard, militarized police, fire hoses, attack dogs, state-sanctioned nightsticks, and more* be made sacrosanct, sacred, inviolable.

Social movements are not armed revolutions. They are not the insurrection of an armed populace against the state. They are something else entirely.

They are the resistance of an unarmed populace against a system of inequity (of *undeserved enrichment* on the backs of *unjust immiseration*).[3] They are the demand for reform, not revolt. They are the use of social pressure, a contest in the public conscience, for a cause that is right and just – the dogged use of civil disobedience through direct action that discomfits power until one's just demands are met. They are the parable of Christ about the persistent widow who troubled the unjust judge until her needs were addressed simply to shut her up.[4]

And, in the same way as with the unjust judge, in a democracy, organized collective action can – and has – and does -- force *elected* officials sit up, take notice, and acquiesce.

About collective action, James Baldwin said, our *"obligation . . . is to examine society and try to change it,"* and to do so, *"no matter"* what the *"risk,"* because *"this is the only hope society has. This is the only way societies change."*[5]

Through the study of social movements, we increase our *empathetic intelligence*, for, to quote Gloria Steinem, *"Empathy is the most revolutionary emotion."*[6] The study of social movements forwards the project of a steadily increasing democratic freedom.

In the project of making a just and compassionate society, each generation of movement activist dies with part of the work still undone, and so, each generation must pass the baton. There must be those, up and coming, who care, who understand where we have been, who have come to consciousness, and who, seeing both the forest and the trees, have an analysis of where we still need to go and the way to get there.

We study social justice movements to pick up the baton.

Social movements fight for justice whether or not it can ever be won.

As Tim Wise has said, *"We should live our lives as if justice"* were *"possible . . . whether or not it is,"*[7] because even though *"there is no . . . place called "Justice,"*[8] there is something redemptive in *"the struggle itself,"* and our *"striving for equality and freedom"* is something our *"very humanity depends"*

8

upon – that *"gives life meaning,"* and through which *"we become [truly] human"*[9] – something that can *"save our lives morally and ethically, if not physically."*[10]

We pick up the baton because, in the words of Archbishop Desmond Tutu, we must *"do the things [we] do because the things [we] are doing are right."*[11]

We pick up the baton because, again, as Tim Wise puts it,

> I have no idea whether anything I say, do, or write will make the least bit of difference in the world. But I say it, do it, and write it anyway, because as uncertain as the outcome of our resistance may be, the outcome of our silence and inaction is anything but. We know exactly what will happen if we don't do the work: nothing. And given that choice, between certainly and promise, in which territory one finds the measure of our resolve and humanity, I will opt for hope.[12]

In the following section, I will discuss the conditions theorists believe allow for the development of social reform movements, as opposed to armed revolutions. Then, I will briefly outline the history of a number of important social justice movements (there are many more I did not cover). And finally, I will focus in on the active LGBTQ (lesbian/gay/bisexual/transgender/queer) movement today and its struggle for equality through recognition of civil marriage rights, without bias against the gender of the partners.

Origins of Social Movements

Collective action has taken place at many times and places throughout recorded history.[13] Early theorists of collective behavior viewed collective action as the dangerous uprising of disgruntled or disaffected mobs[14] and often used a social psychological lens to theorize about the behavior of crowds.[15]

Mass society theorists viewed the outbreak of collective action as undesirable and the result of a rupture in the system.[16]

This view shifted as theorists turned their focus to the identity movements of the mid-20th century. The compelling nature of the social justice claims of the mid-century movements,[17] and the change in the academy as former student activists became scholars, caused a shift in perspective.[18] Research questions shifted from *how to prevent* mass uprisings to *how to incite and maintain* them.[19]

Social justice movements cannot exist outside of the right constellation of social forces. We can date the beginning of the kind of collective action we identify as typical of a social justice movement to the end of the 18th century – within democracies.[20]

In part, social justice movements arise within the structural conditions of the democratic nation state, because at the same time as nationalism promotes the creation of associative networks beyond regional locales, democratic ideology encourages the formation of an identity – as a ***citizen*** – in a *participatory* and *self-governing* collective.[21]

Another piece of the puzzle in the production of a social justice movement, is that there must be a balance between *oppression* (a grievance that becomes the base of a social justice demand), and the *liberty* to engage in collective action (at a calculated risk) – a balance between a lack of inclusion in the democracy or a lack of fair treatment (grievance) – and the resources necessary (shared symbols/time/and associational and communication networks) – to press a social movement claim.[22]

Political process theorists argue that shifts in social forces (or history effects) allow excluded groups to:

1.) see the possibility of inclusion,

2.) gather together in networks, and

3.) press their claims for social inclusion and reform.[23]

Identity-based associative networks connect individuals and groups beyond regional locales, and are necessary as a constituent base from which to draw and mobilize recruits.[24] Theorists emphasize the importance of the "existence of social ties among potential recruits" – the importance of the "social networks through which people are mobilized."[25]

It is possible for "organizers . . . [to] set about building a new network suited to their own purposes . . . , [but it] takes longer than mobilizing or co-opting an existing network."[26] Identity communities with ""dense" ties, or preexisting formal organizations . . . find it easier to mobilize supporters, and build a movement," since "emotions . . . are the real life blood of networks," and "people respond to the information they receive through networks, because of [their] affective ties to those in the network."[27]

An expanded national (and increasingly, global) sense of these associational ties began with the rise of the nation state and its concurrent increase in communication.[28] Just as people began to think of themselves in terms of expanded collectivities, printing became inexpensive enough to allow the relatively wide distribution of pamphlets and newspapers (a function now even further expanded by the internet). This new ability to communicate across associational networks began to be put to good use in forwarding social movement claims by the late 18th century.[29]

Organization

While "organizations usually play a part," social movements are made up of ordinary people rather than "army officers, politicians, or economic elites."[30] Social movements function by mobilizing a loose affiliative network of potential constituents to undertake direct, collective action for a particular social movement claim. This often happens through the leadership of social movement organizations (SMOs). However, SMOs are not movements in and of themselves, and social movements often exist without top down organization and may "in a traditional sense" be "leaderless."[31] Social movements may be made up of "coalition[s] of hundreds of groups . . . formed by thousands of organizers" without even a "premier organization" to "set the agenda."[32]

Repertoire

Social movements exist outside of, and distinct from, the ordinary operation of an electoral and legislative democracy. They challenge "authorities and powerholders," in a "sustained manner," with the claims of the socially and/or politically marginalized.[33] They are extra-institutional, in that they seek to make change from the outside in, through what we call the "social movement repertoire."[34]

The social movement repertoire is a particular set of direction action strategies, meant to attract attention to the social movement claim, until the demands of the movement are met. These tactics include mass meetings, street demonstrations, rallies, strikes, sit-ins, boycotts, and disruptions of commerce and routine daily activities.[35] Both movements, and movement leaders, must make choices between kinds of tactics: "violent and nonviolent," "illegal and legal," "disrupt[ive] and education[al]," extreme[ist] and moderat[e]."[36]

Movements Within Movements

Liberal/Radical

Along with strategic choices about tactics, social movement adherents also make choices between perspectives. Many, if not most, U.S. social movements separate within-group along a liberal/radical divide. Within a larger movement, different sectors may argue different premises.

On one side, movement sectors may argue their essential sameness with a mainstream norm, and demand their inclusion in the privileges of the status quo as their "right ("civil rights"). On the other side, another sector may argue its essential difference from mainstream norms and demand – either freedom from adherence to those norms, or its need for different protections and freedoms.

These critical choices may cause enough division to foster the argument that they are actually different movements: one liberal, the other radical; one assimilationist, the other separatist.[37]

A case in point is feminist movements. Some first-wave feminists argued the essential sameness of "woman"[38] with "man,"[39] as the grounds for the inclusion of women[40] in the citizenship rights accorded to (White) men. Others argued that women were different from men and were, therefore, both morally superior (and hence, even more deserving of suffrage), and at the same time, more fragile (and hence, deserving of special protections—including workplace protections, and prohibition, as protection from drunken husbands).

In addition, second-wave feminists began by arguing for full inclusion in the male worlds of education and employment, with equal access and equal wages, resulting in the branch of the movement represented by the National Organization of Women (NOW); while younger feminists, conscious of their gendered mistreatment within the other movements of the time took a more radical approach, demanding not so much an equality with men in all-male preserves – but separatist women's spaces—up to and including, separatist (and thus, lesbian)

15

bedroom space (Lavender Menace; Radicalesbians; The Furies Collective; Lesbian Feminists).

Another case in point is the Black movement for Civil Rights in the 1960s and 70s, as it divided over the demand for integration and the Black Nationalist demand for separatism.

Also, the movement for lesbian, gay, bisexual, transgender, and queer (LGBTQ) civil rights began with the liberal demand of the Homophile Movement of the 1950s and 1960s for individual and self-acceptance, and was radicalized as homophile efforts at community building and coming out met younger LGBTQ activists (groomed in the Anti-War, Feminist, Black Civil Rights, and New Left movements), who responded to the Stonewall Rebellion by the spontaneous generation of the essentially-disconnected, grassroots, cells of the early Gay Liberation Movement.

The severity of the AIDS Crisis further radicalized the movement, with the demand for government aid and medical research to abate the epidemic, led by SMOs like ACT-UP; even as it concurrently ramped up the relatively-less-radical (or perceptually-more-heteronormative and somewhat-more-liberal) demand for increased monogamy (as a form of safer sex) with same-sex/same-gender marriage equality, and SMOs like Marriage Equality, U.S.A., and a host of state-by-state equality organization (like Garden State Equality, Equality Pennsylvania, Equality California, etc.).

Political/Cultural

Within their liberal/radical (and assimilationist/separatist) divides, movements again subdivide into the political and the cultural. Movement actors do not only press their demands in the political sphere. After the consciousness of the group is raised, the publishing abroad of their social movement claims has an effect on the general consciousness of the mainstream society, so that whatever changes may (or may not) be enacted in the political and legal sphere – change happens in the cultural as well.

Women don't just get included as a protected category in the 1964 Civil Rights Act. Many people across the populace come to see the social movement demand for women's equality as rational and natural, and movement claims about women's access to public spaces (education and the workplace), and the need to end violence against women, as serious and valid.

African Americans don't simply win enforcement of voting rights or desegregation of public transportation. However intractable, racism comes to be seen (sometimes even by its adherents) as illegitimate and untenable, and expressions of racist sentiment (even though far from non-existent) are publicly modified (become "politically incorrect").

Social movement activism educates and raises the consciousness of constituents and the culture at large, creates solidarity among constituents, modifies cultural symbols, and rewrites the characters and scripts of the sociopolitical discourse.[41]

U.S. SOCIAL MOVEMENTS

Historical Developments

The United States itself could be viewed as born in social movement. The colonial rebellion against the tariffs of the English monarchy was forwarded by an increasing sense of nationalism, and by increased access to communication across affiliative networks (the cheap printing of pamphlets advocating resistance, and or, revolution).[42]

The rise of democracy, and the nation state, allowed structurally for the channeling of collective discontent into the outlet of social movements. History effects (like industrialization, deindustrialization, food technologies, information technologies, the advent of nuclear weapons, increases and decreases in prosperity, and more) affected shifts in the course and profusion – or dearth of – social movements.[43]

The profusion of movements at mid-20th century must be seen in the "context of the larger history of . . . post World War II."[44] With World War II, the United States went from being a globally uninvolved nation of small, mostly rural, communities, to a world superpower in a global arms race. The federal government consolidated power and became more intrusive in the daily lives of Americans.[45]

> Macro-economists, public policy analysts, foreign area experts, marketing specialists, and education consultants – a whole class of professional people . . . exploded after World War II – entered the corridors of power and rethought the capacities of the federal government . . . universities, business corporations, and

other large-scale institutions, in order to shape daily life in . . . the world."[46]

The "unprecedented" "material comfort" of the post-war period, following as it did, hard upon the heels of the deprivation of the Great Depression and the rationing of the war years, had a significant effect upon American consciousness.[47] "Many Americans . . . feared the centralized, expert-oriented, and bureaucratized kind of society that America was becoming,"[48] and post-war America remained an armed, military state, with its hand on its holster. The rhetoric and fear of the Cold War, with its air raid drills and its Cuban Missile crisis and its standing military/industrial complex, had a profound effect on the generation that came of age during the Vietnam War and the civil rights era.[49] This same cohort experienced the assassination of one president, one presidential candidate, and many Black rights leaders (including Rev. Dr. King, Malcolm X, and a number of prominent Black Panthers).[50]

In addition, American media had changed. Affected by the war, it had become less regional and more national in emphasis, and a new form of media had a profound impact. "Television . . . out of New York City produced a different kind of news and thus a different kind of informed citizenry than did newspaper editors in homogeneous communities."[51] Through nationalized media, the cultural production of "values" became more homogeneous as well. It also became easier to circumvent local bigotries and press your social movement claim to parts of the populace who might not know, and who might, in some measure, be made to care.[52]

Abolition

The first stirrings of the abolitionist movement began, even before the Revolutionary War, in religion. While still an agrarian economy, except for the impetus to separate from England, there were relatively few social movements in the American colonies, and the early United States, that were not religiously-based. In 1688 (ninety-two years before Pennsylvania became the first state to outlaw slavery in 1780), a group of Quakers in Germantown, Pennsylvania,[53] signed and published a written protest calling for the abolition of slavery.[54] The freeborn African American street planner for Washington, D.C., Benjamin Banneker, routinely published anti-slavery material in his almanac. In 1791, he began an ongoing correspondence with then-Secretary of State Thomas Jefferson, arguing against slavery and racial subjugation.[55] Rebellions against slavery occurred from the start of the "peculiar institution," including: the New York City slave rebellion of 1712, Gabriel Prosser's planned revolt in 1800, Denmark Vesey's attempt at insurrection in 1821, Nat Turner's rebellion in 1831, the Amistad mutiny in 1839, and the Christiana Resistance of 1851.[56] And individual slaves, both African and American born, resisted in a myriad of daily ways, and by escape, either North – as in the journey north that became known as the Underground Railroad, or South or West – to refuge with Native peoples.

In 1831, William Lloyd Garrison began publication of *The Liberator*, a social movement publication dedicated to abolition.[57] Also by the 1830s, both Black[58] and White[59] activists had begun to dedicate themselves to the social movement claim. By the late 1840s/early 1850s, Harriet Tubman and William Still became active in the movement. With the passage of the Fugitive Slave Act in 1850, the level of terror increased. Not only did it become necessary for escaped slaves to continue to Canada, but in the North, pro-slavery mobs rioted against abolitionist lecturers and meetings until almost the end of the Civil War.[60]

Abolitionists formed social movement organizations, like the national American Anti-slavery Society, the Female Anti-slavery Society, and many state-based societies. They made skillful use of media and loose networks of association to persuade potential constituents of the correctness of their social movement claims. Even though ending slavery did not end racial injustice, abolitionism ended in the successful resolution of their social movement claim – the emancipation of the slaves through the Northern victory in the Civil War.

Labor

The labor movement in the United States began even before industrialization, in Revolutionary times, in craft guilds. Guilds provided the networks of association essential to collective action,[61] and allowed for the use of the social movement repertoire tactic of labor strikes. The shift from cottage industry to factory labor then led to the application of these techniques in the mills and mines.

By 1836, the mill girls of Lowell Massachusetts organized a strike to resist a cut in pay.[62] They were unsuccessful in stopping management from reducing their wages but inspired others to agitate for change. The Great Strike of 1877 also demonstrated the power of labor to resist.[63]

On the outside, labor movements struggled with management, capital, and not infrequently, with government. The fourteen-month strike of [12,000] coal miners – that culminated in the Ludlow Massacre of 1914 – shows the growing use of organized collective action against, and the response of those in, power.[64]

On the inside, labor movements often divided along lines of race and gender, pitting laborer against laborer along fissures of subgroup interest. This was shown in the Uprising of the 20,000 in November 1909 – organized (and even led) by young (often only teenage) Jewish and Italian immigrant women – and toward which male labor movements initially showed little interest.[65] Even though the strike (part of which targeted the Triangle Shirtwaist Company) did not keep Triangle's owners from locking their fire exits (before or after the tragedy), the deaths (a little over a year after the strike, in March of 1911) of 146 of these young women strikers[66] in the Triangle Shirtwaist Company fire[67] was the genesis of the International Ladies Garment Workers Union. That strike also – punctuated as it was by the avoidable deaths of young girls – increased public acceptance of the justice of labor movement claims, had a profound effect on public and governmental consciousness about the needs of labor, and changed New York State labor laws – demonstrating the effectiveness of the social movement repertoire of the growing labor movement.[68]

In its inception, the American labor movement was not in any way a part of a bureaucracy. It was the collectivization of oppressed groups, gathered around shared working and living conditions, and pressing their social movement claims to those in power, as demands for change. And, for a time at least, the American labor movement made tremendous improvements in the conditions of the American working class, securing reasonable work hours and a living wage, and allowing, in the post-World War II period,[69] for the rise of much of the working class into middle class status.

It is beyond the province of this work to fully explicate the history of the labor movement, unionization and/or socialism in the United States. However, as Howard Zinn notes, the "most essential character" of even our present day "economic system" is "the control of the lives of working people by powerful, invisible forces."[70] U.S. government and multinational corporate policies continue to affect the lives of the poor, working poor, working, and middle class throughout the United States and around the globe.[71] With federal policy contributing to corporate incentives to outsource once-unionized jobs overseas, "production . . . becom[ing] less pivotal . . . [and] capital flee[ing] the country in search of cheaper labor, relatively lower taxes, and a deregulated, frequently anti-union environment," the struggle between labor and capital and government continues.[72] In this changing environment, "the renewed labor movement" in the U.S. has refocused on the economic strata that remains – the "service-based economy."[73] This includes "healthcare . . . education . . . office building maintenance, telemarketing, food processing, food service . . . retail . . . and the prison-industrial complex."[74] These new jobs are increasingly

23

raced, gendered, and insufficient for sustenance (underpaid, part-time, and lacking in benefits). The new labor movement is also, of necessity, refocusing "beyond the boundaries of the nation-state," as "any significant challenge to global capital" must "depend . . . on international solidarity."[75] And any true movement for international solidarity around laborer's rights must take into account the global rise of enslaved and trafficked labor.[76]

Progressive Reform Movements

Other movements of the time include the reformation of child labor laws, and the public education movement. Along with raising the educational prospects for children, the public education movement also increased the availability of wage labor for women outside the home, as primary and, eventually, secondary school teachers. Progressive reformers also worked to alleviate the poverty and disease in immigrant neighborhoods, opened clinics, taught hygiene, advocated for birth control, opened settlement houses, and advocated temperance as a measure against domestic violence.[77] Progressive reformers also founded schools for the emancipated slaves, and with undesirable results, for the children of Native American tribes.

First-Wave Women's Rights Activism

Many of the Progressive reform movements were female-founded and female-led, offshoots of first-wave feminism. The feminist movement was born among women, largely Quaker, who were, first, active abolitionists. Lucretia Coffin Mott and Elizabeth Cady Stanton met at the *World Anti-Slavery Convention* in London in 1840. Both attended the convention as authorized representatives of anti-slavery societies, Mott having founded the first *Female Anti-Slavery Society*.[78] In London, only a handful of women were in attendance, and the male delegates refused to allow them a seat on the floor. Instead, they were forced to spend the convention behind a curtain in a gallery,[79] while the men on the floor below them debated their presence.[80]

The experience drove home the connection between their own social and legal positions, and those of the slaves they labored to liberate. At the beginning of the first-wave, a woman did not exist, legally. Guardianship of her was transferred from father to husband at marriage. If she was heir to any property, it became her husband's at marriage, and he could use or dispose of it without her knowledge or consent. A woman had no right to enact contracts, sue or be sued, sit on a jury, or initiate any form of legal action in the courts. Following the British Common Law doctrine of *Coverture*, unless concurrently orphaned, adult, and unmarried, a woman was always under the "covering" of one man, and her title of address (Miss or Mrs.) and surname indicated which man owned her – father or husband.[81] Her person, her labor, her services, (in marriage, her children), and even the clothes on her back and her personal effects, were property of that one man as well.

The same ideological connections were being drawn at about the same time by other female anti-slavery lecturers, including Sarah and Angelina Grimke, Lucy Stone, and Susan B. Anthony; each of whom broke restrictive social convention against women by speaking in public (in mixed gender assemblies)[82] in order to advance the cause of the abolition of slavery.[83]

Mott and Stanton determined to do something about their own, and women's, conditions and subsequently held the first women's rights convention in Seneca Falls, NY in July 1848. At that convention, with only the support of Frederick Douglass, Cady Stanton (who penned the Declaration of Rights and Sentiments, with opening paragraphs modeled on the Declaration of Independence) proposed adding the demand for suffrage. Other platforms included women's social and legal equality with, and autonomy from, men, and the opening to women of higher education, the professions, business, and the ministry.

The first-wave of feminism lasted 72 years, from 1848 to 1920, falling from public (and media) view after the suffrage amendment was ratified. Women had won their legal existence,[84] including: the right to retain ownership of property after marriage, the right to their own person/ labor/ wages/ and personal effects, the right to full or joint custody of their children, the right to inherit a husband's property, and the right to sue, including for divorce.

A steady trickle of class- and race-privileged women entered college and pressed into business and the professions (though, unless forced by economics, mothers of young children still withdrew from the public sphere). The women who began the movement died off before the vote was won, many of them having dedicated 40, 50, or more, years to the cause. The torch was carried forward by a second and third generation of younger activists. But even though many issues of inequality remained unaddressed, once suffrage was won, grassroots activism died out and feminism left the public eye for almost four and a half decades.

In "the doldrums,"[85] some of the younger activists powered on. Alice Paul founded the National Woman Party and formulated the Equal Rights Amendment. She saw that it was submitted to Congress annually from 1923 until its passage in 1972 (the Equal Rights Amendment, however, fell three states short of ratification, and did not become law). Through the Depression of the 1930s, the global convulsion of World War II, and the retro repression of the "idyllic" post-war 1950s and 60s, handfuls of women continued their activism in the NWP and in the League of Women Voters.

African American Movements

There is no actual break in Black activism between the end of the abolitionist movement, at the end of the Civil War, and the emergence of the public wave of activism we now recognize as the Civil Rights Movement. There has always been Black resistance to oppression. From the beginning of the African Diaspora – and on this land mass, from the beginning of the American colonies and continuing through the history of the United States, up to the present day – there has always been as much organized Black resistance to oppression as has been humanly possible.

Throughout the decades, during the media-silence between the waves of media-visible activism, there have always been dedicated activists pressing for change and growing Black social movement organizations (SMOs). Beyond the limelight, they have founded and forwarded legal, religious, and educational civil rights initiatives. So, whether or not they garnered White-dominated, power structure (or media) attention, there was ongoing Black collective action and Black forward motion in the hundred-year span between abolition and civil rights.

The abolition of slavery did not change the ideology of the majority of Whites.

In Southern states, under slavery, all adult males were required to take turns patrolling the fields and woods as "paddy rollers," looking for runaways. When, at the end of Reconstruction (1865-1877), the North withdrew its troops from the South, to send them West, to

28

finish off the forced relocation of Native Americans (through the genocidal massacres misnamed the "Indian Wars") – these trained slave catchers formed the genesis of the Ku Klux Klan – intent on reinstating what they could of the Southern (Whites in dominion) "way of life."[86]

The South also passed laws to maintain "the separation of the races" (de jure' segregation), while the North simply enforced the same separation without Jim Crow laws (de facto segregation).

The newly-arrived Southern and Eastern European immigrants, and the Catholic famine-Irish (not originally seen as White) competed with the newly-emancipated slaves, who had been set free and set adrift – without education, training, or resources – at the bottom of the socioeconomic ladder.

The new, voluntary, immigrants fought to press into being considered White,[87] pointing out the similarity between the color of their own skin and the color of the skin of those native-born Whites from whom they sought employ. At the same time, native-born African American "freedmen" and freedwomen[88] whose ancestors had been brought here involuntarily, and who had labored here for generations, were terrorized by the Klan, kept segregated (read: "isolated") by law, and often forced – by economics – to accept re-absorption into the revamped slavery-related systems of share-cropping (tenant farming) and domestic servitude[89] or – by discriminatory policing – into the system of convict labor peonage.[90]

Leaders – from Sojourner Truth at the end of the Civil War, to Marcus Garvey in the 1920s, to Malcolm X and other Black Nationalists in the late 1960s and 70s – set the goal as self-determination, and demanded, either in America or in Africa, land on which to build their own nation.[91]

In the approximate seventy years between the end of Reconstruction (1877) and the (post-World War II) Civil Rights Movement, Black social and educational organizations were empowered by the ideology of "lifting as we climb" (the ideal of striving for individual and group achievement with an eye on "uplifting" the race).[92] Black leaders, like Booker T. Washington and W.E.B. DuBois, even though divided in perspective and strategy, mutually sought the best way to 'advance the race.'

In 1896, as a means of group empowerment, Black women organized the SMO, *The National Association of Colored Women* (NACW) to "uplift" the race." Their social movement organizing was a "response to a vicious attack on the character of African-American women by a Southern journalist," and to "disfranchisement,[93] lynching,[94] and segregation." They grew NACW, from its start in Washington D.C., into a national Black women's club movement.

> The organization's founders included some of the most renowned African-American women educators, community leaders, and civil rights activists . . . including: Harriet Tubman, Frances E. W. Harper, Josephine St. Pierre Ruffin, Margaret Murray Washington, Ida B. Wells-Barnett, and Mary Church Terrell. . . .[95]

In 1909, the SMO, *The National Association for the Advancement of Colored People* (NAACP) was formed as a legal arm of Black forward movement.[96] The interracial board of the NAACP sought test cases that could be prosecuted up the judicial docket to the U.S. Supreme

Court. Their greatest victory came in 1954, when *Brown v. Board of Education*[97] brought the legal (though still not fully realized) end of school segregation.

The branch of the Black movement that we call *the Civil Rights Movement* made use of a full range of social movement repertoire strategies, and with the influence of Bayard Rustin[98] (himself a protégé of A.J. Muste), and the Rev. Dr. Martin Luther King, Jr., elevated non-violent direct action to a new level.[99] *Brown v. Board* (1954), and the *Montgomery Bus Boycott* (December 1, 1955 through December 20, 1956), jumpstarted this period of media visibility (1955-1968), in which the majority of legal advances, that have been won, were won.

Black migration North also supplied the movement with "more resources and denser social ties," allowing for more [visible] mobilization . . . [and] raised expectations, causing rapid growth from Brown onward.[100] Through the use of non-violent confrontation, movement strategists sought to use national media to reach beyond the entrenched resistance of local Southern Whites, to the relatively-less-racist conscience of Northern White liberals. The *Civil Rights* branch of the movement forwarded the liberal demand for integration – for full access to the range of establishment rights and privileges.

These victories, and other public actions, and advances, set off firestorms of White racist backlash in both the South and the North.

1. In the de facto segregation of the North, the backlash centered on anger over busing for school integration. (More than fifty years later, most U.S. public primary and secondary schools still remain largely segregated – by means of assigning attendance by neighborhood – reflecting ongoing racial residential segregation).[101]

31

2. In the aftermath of the deposed, de jure' segregation of the South – rather than integrate – White backlash shut down entire, statewide, public school systems for more than a year at a time.[102]

But with the outcome of Brown v. Board, the Montgomery Bus Boycott became possible. Yet, to have a more complete understanding of the movement to integrate public accommodations – to end (de jure' and de facto) segregation – we must situation these events in their historical antecedents, for our purposes, specifically in the demand for transportation integration.[103]

Black men – and women – had been refusing to give up their seats on public transportation for as long as there had been public transportation (dating back to horse-drawn stagecoaches and trolleys, steamships and passenger trains).[104] (In fact, the fight began with the demand for mere access to public conveyances. The first *segregated* railroad cars and seating sections were a corporate concession, *won in response to protests*, begun at least as early as 1835, by free Blacks in the North who were initially denied the right to be transported at all.)[105]

To address the issue, the Black community around the country engaged, wherever possible, in "litigation and local organizing."[106] By 1838:

> Incidents of Blacks being forcibly removed from Boston and Providence trains for refusing to sit in segregated cars were frequently reported in Massachusetts newspapers. . . . Abolitionists encouraged boycotts . . . and free Blacks began seeking help before the Massachusetts state legislature. . . . [107]

In 1841, on July 6th, a free Black abolitionist, by the name of David Ruggles,[108] "boarded one of the regular cars of the New Bedford and Taunton Rail Road" and was "ordered by the conductor" to go to the segregated car. When he refused, he "was dragged from the coach by the conductor and several other train employees, his clothing [was] torn in the scuffle," and he "was thrown unceremoniously out onto the depot platform." Ruggles sued the railroad "for assault and battery," and abolitionists helped organize "a mass protest meeting." (The judge, a stockholder in the railroad, found in favor of the railroad corporation and dismissed the case.)[109]

Also in 1841, in September, "a light-colored Black woman," who was Secretary of the Massachusetts Anti-Slavery Society,[110] was dragged – baby in arms – from a railroad car, for refusing to move. The infant was injured, as was her husband, who tried to defend her.[111]

In his autobiography, Frederick Douglass delineates the "repeated clashes" he had in Massachusetts, with railroad car segregation.[112] Douglass said:

> My treatment in the use of public conveyances about these times was really rough. . . . There was a mean, dirty, and uncomfortable car set apart for colored travelers called the Jim Crow car. Regarding this as the fruit of slaveholding prejudice, and being determined to fight the spirit of slavery wherever I might find it, I resolved to avoid this car, though it sometimes required some courage to do so. . . . Sometimes [I] was soundly beaten by conductor and brakeman. On one occasion six of these 'fellows of the baser sort,' under the direction of the conductor, set out to eject me from my seat. As usual, I had purchased a first-class ticket and paid the required sum for it, and on the requirement of the conductor to leave, refused to do so, when he called

on these men to 'snake me out.' They attempted to obey with an air which plainly told me they relished the job. They however found me much attached to my seat, and In removing me I tore away two or three of the surrounding ones, on which I held with a firm grasp, and did the car no service in some other respects."(17-18)[113]

In 1843 – 7 years before the Fugitive Slave Act of 1850, 18 years before the start of the Civil War in 1861, and 22 years before the end of the Civil War in 1865 – Black passengers and abolitionists offered enough organized and ongoing resistance to transportation segregation that Massachusetts enacted a bill mandating that:

> No railroad corporation in the commonwealth of Massachusetts should make distinctions in accommodations based on a passenger's descent, sect or color, and further stipulated that any "officer or servant" of a railroad who assaulted a rider in an attempt to remove him from his seat for reasons of ancestry, sect or color would be jailed for not less than six days or fined not less than ten dollars, and that the corporation would be liable to the full amount of any damages incurred by the assaulted passenger.[114]

In 1865, Sojourner Truth led a public and personal fight for the desegregation of horse-drawn streetcars in Washington, D.C. As a public figure, well known to abolitionists and supporters of slavery alike, she intentionally put herself in harm's way to "focus attention" on "the injustice of segregation" and "encourage[d] other Blacks to ride the horse cars" in the spirit of resistance.[115]

First, she had to fight to be allowed on the streetcars, in that Truth "often found herself ignored by drivers when she tried to get them to stop" to let her board.[116] Determined, she would do her best to force drivers to allow her to ride, even chasing trolleys that passed her by, verbally shaming the conductors when she caught them.[117] Once on board and seated, "if a driver . . . told [her] to sit in the Jim Crow car with . . . the other Black passengers"[118] she, routinely, refused to give up her seat and "acted boldly,"[119] 'risking humiliation' and "her physical safety."[120] She insisted she would sit "where she pleased; not where she was told."[121] Once, while traveling in "the company of" Michigan abolitionist Laura Haviland, Truth was slammed against a door by a conductor, and received a bruised right shoulder."[122] Truth and Haviland "reported the incident to the president of the streetcar company."[123] "He promptly dismissed the conductor."[124] This was "the second conductor Truth had caused to be dismissed."[125] Through her repeated resistances, and those she was able to inspire,[126] Truth was able "to have the Jim Crow car removed from the Washington D. C. system."[127]

In 1870, the Black community challenged segregation on the Central Passenger Line in Louisville, KY. On October 30th, Horace Pearce and (brothers) Robert and Samuel Fox, boarded and took seats. Whites mobbed the trolley. The three Black men were arrested for disorderly conduct, and the Louisville Black community "boycotted the company all winter."[128] Robert Fox sued, won, and was "awarded . . . $15,"[129] thereby winning "the right to ride the city's streetcars without restriction" for "Louisville's African American citizens."[130]

The 1896 U.S. Supreme Court *Plessy v. Ferguson* case, which "sustained the constitutionality of Louisiana's Jim Crow law," was a case about resistance to segregation in intrastate travel.[131] The *Plessy* ruling, affirming segregation, was surrounded by much Black resistance to the lies of "separate but equal." At the end of the 19th, and in the early 20th centuries, African Americans "boycotted streetcar lines in more than twenty-seven cities," "fac[ing] down the violence of lynching and urban [White-initiated] race riots."[132]

> In 1890 a new Louisiana law required railroads to provide "equal but separate accommodations for the White, and colored, races." Outraged, the Black community in New Orleans decided to test the rule.
>
> On June 7, 1892, Homer Plessy agreed to be arrested for refusing to move from a seat reserved for Whites. Judge John H. Ferguson upheld the law, and the case of *Plessy v. Ferguson* slowly moved up to the Supreme Court.
>
> On May 18, 1896, the U.S. Supreme Court, with only one dissenting vote, ruled that segregation in America was constitutional. [A ruling that stood until Brown v. Board of Education of Topeka, 347 U.S. (1954).][133]

Montgomery, Alabama, itself:

> witnessed a boycott of Jim Crow [transportation] lines that lasted for two years, from 1900 to 1902. And although the local transportation companies gave in to the boycotters' demands, segregated seating was soon reinstated through city ordinances.[134]

We are not able to begin to name all of those who resisted, or organized against, segregation in transportation in the almost hundred year span between Truth and Parks, but we know it happened countless times.

Another resistance, followed by successful protest, of which I am aware was undertaken in Pennsylvania. From 1859, a local Philadelphia "protest movement" was "brewing" around the "possibilities" of "racial integration," and around the possibilities of "break[ing] the color line,"[135] and that, "most immediately, on the streetcars."[136]

In 1861, Black abolitionist William Still drew "up a petition in favor of the right to ride the cars" and made an estimated "1000" visits "to bankers, editors, judges, merchants, ministers, lawyers and other civic leaders," asking for their help and their signatures on the petition.[137] By 1862, Still "had gathered the signatures of some 360 prominent Philadelphians, including Quakers who would ride on the [segregated] front platform [of the streetcar] in solidarity." In a letter to the Editor of the National Anti-Slavery Standard, Alfred H. Love reported, "Some of us had refused to ride for nearly a year. . . . Some made the sacrifice to ride on the front platform . . . and even in storms, our dear friend Lucretia Mott, now so ill, has taken her stand beside them in that exposed position." [138]

> At the very hour Congress adopt[ed] the 13th Amendment [1865], officially ending slavery [in the South] – [in the North] in Philadelphia, street car operators polled their exclusively White riders. Would they accept Black riders? [Their] answer [was], "No." The tally, 20 to 1. . . .

More Black resistance followed:

> Later that year, a lone woman [defied] the rule. She [boarded] a streetcar. When she [was] told to leave, she [refused].

37

As instructed [by the street car company], the horses [were] detached [by the driver]. The White riders [moved] to another car.

The woman [sat] there, by herself, for twenty-four hours.

At the same time, Caroline LeCount (a "brilliant orator," a teacher at *The Institute for Colored Youth,* and "an outspoken campaigner for equal rights"), Octavius Catto, ("also a teacher at *The Institute"),* and William Still, Black abolitionist and conductor/station master on the Underground Railroad, "pushed hard" for legislation[139] to mandate "equal access" for Black riders on the statewide streetcar system.[140]

Against even Black pressure, Still, Catto, and LeCount[141] proposed, pushed, and "lobbied" in Harrisburg, for a year and a half, for "passage of a streetcar desegregation" bill, to "integrate streetcars across the state."[142] On March 22, 1867, the Pennsylvania Legislature passed an act prohibiting discrimination" on local and state trolley and railroad lines."[143]

Concurrent with that 1867 legislation, the case, "*West Chester and Philadelphia Railroad Company v. Miles* came before the [Pennsylvania] Supreme Court."

> At issue was a rule of the company that required blacks to sit at one end of the company's cars. Mrs. Vera Miles, an African-American passenger, refused to comply with the law by selecting a seat toward the middle of the day coach, an area designated for white passengers only. When she refused to move after a stern warning by the conductor, she was ejected from the car. Mrs. Miles sued the railroad," won, and was

"awarded . . . damages."[144]

On the ground, the new legislation, and the new court ruling, had to be tested and, then, exercised.

Catto and LeCount determined to "test the new law." On March 25, 1867, LeCount tried to "board a streetcar at 11th and Lombard" streets.[145] Not unlike with Sojourner Truth, the driver ignored her, and the streetcar kept moving, without granting her entrance.

The driver shouted, *"We don't allow n_____ to ride."* LeCount went to the court, which initially "refuse[d] to hear the case." So LeCount "obtain[ed] a copy of the law," "return[ed] to [the] court," was heard, and the magistrate awarded "a one hundred dollar penalty," significant "by the standards of the day"[146] Thus, public transportation was desegregated for Black Philadelphians – as passengers.

Despite LeCount, Catto, and Still's success with passage and enforcement of the streetcar desegregation bill, jobs in Philadelphia's public transportation company remained segregated another 80 years.

The positioning of Philadelphia, during World War II, as "a major U.S. war production center"[147] created "a vast demand" for local labor and mandated a "kind of suspension of the old rules," that opened industrial jobs to women of all colors and to African American men.[148]

Suburbanization, highway construction programs, and the massive boom in the automobile industry were all post-war social forces. Prior to and during the war, Philadelphia-area workers relied heavily:

> on a massive network of streetcars and subways to
> reach their jobs at defense plants across the city, but at

the *Philadelphia Transportation Company (PTC)*, the job of trolley operator [was] for Whites only.[149]

The *PTC* consigned Black workers to janitorial, track-laying, mechanical, or porters' roles.[150] A "major force in" the Philadelphia NAACP and its first executive secretary, local civil rights leader, Carolyn Davenport Moore,[151] grew that SMO to 7,000 members, then led them in a campaign against "the discriminatory practices" of the PTC,[152] – including a protest by African American PTC employees – demanding "equal opportunity."[153]

They won a "federal order requiring the company to integrate its workforce and treat Blacks more equitably."[154]

> Whites, and the [Transportation Workers'] Union, were furious . . . [and] in August 1944, with fighting intensifying overseas, more than 6,000 White *PTC* workers def[ied] the federal order. They [went out on] strike, shutting down the system, bringing war production to a halt. . . .

Desperate for the munitions' production that had been stopped, Roosevelt "intervened," sending in "troops . . . to run the trains," and threatening anyone who failed to "show up for work" with being immediately drafted and sent into combat. "The federal threat, and military presence" brought an end to the walk out, and Roosevelt "ordered the *PTC* to promote . . . Black workers to be trolley drivers."[155] With the leadership of Carolyn Moore, the Philadelphia NAACP had integrated *PTC* jobs.

Also in 1944, although interstate travel was "supposed to be desegregated," Irene Morgan was arrested in Virginia "for

40

refusing to sit in a segregated section on an interstate Greyhound bus." Morgan "appealed her case," first to the federal court, and finally to the U.S. Supreme Court [*Irene Morgan v. Commonwealth of Virginia*, 328 U.S. 373 (1946)], which "resulted in a landmark ruling" that "state law enforcing segregation on interstate buses was illegal [under] the Equal Protection clause of the *14th Amendment . . .* and *the Interstate Commerce Clause.*"[156]

The Morgan case became the impetus for the 1947 *Journey of Reconciliation*. Sixteen "activists from the Chicago-based" SMO, the *"Congress of Racial Equality"* (CORE) "divided themselves" between *Greyhound* and *Trailways* buses. They then sat in mixed-raced-pairings, together, and rode across state lines. In Virginia, they met with mob violence and arrest. In North Carolina, civil rights activist and leader, Bayard Rustin, was arrested and sentenced by jury "to 22 days on a chain gang." The Journey of Reconciliation "inspired" the "Freedom Rides of 1961, also organized by CORE" and was "ahead of its time in the use of" the tactics of "nonviolent direct actions" – in good measure, because of the leadership of Bayard Rustin, an authority in non-violent civil disobedience.[157]

Also in the 1940s, we know that in 1949, Professor Jo Ann Gibson Robinson, M.A., then of Alabama State College in Montgomery, was accosted on a Montgomery city bus, and determined to organize a boycott to protest the treatment of African Americans on public transportation.[158] In 1950, Professor Robinson became president of the local SMO, the *Women's Political Council* (WPC), and set their agenda to look for the right circumstance with which to spark a bus boycott.[159]

We also know that on March 2, 1955, nine months before the Parks case, 15½ year-old, pregnant, Claudette Colvin, was arrested for refusing to give up her seat on a bus in Montgomery.[160] Pregnant, unmarried, and young, Colvin did not make the "poster" case, for the planned WPC boycott, provided nine months later by the married, settled, Rosa Parks. (Colvin, however, went on to become one of the plaintiffs – along with Aurelia Shines Browder Coleman (Apr 1955)[161], Susie McDonald, and Mary Louise Smith Ware (Oct 1955)[162] – in the1956 civil rights class-action lawsuit, *Browder v. Gayle*, which culminated in the December 17, 1956 United States Supreme Court ruling that ended segregation on local public transportation.)[163]

Arrested on December 1, 1955, besides being married, Mrs. Rosa Parks (a savvy political activist)[164] was impeccably upstanding, publicly demure, hardworking, and secretary of the Montgomery NAACP.

Literally overnight, Professor Robinson and the *Women's Political Council* went into action, hand-mimeographing and distributing 35,000 flyers, calling for a boycott.[165] They distributed the handbills through the Black church and school networks,[166] and with the success of the initial boycott, the local minister's council sought the young Martin Luther King, Jr. as their figurehead (in part, because his newness in town meant he had escaped corruption by local White political leaders), and on December 5, 1955, formed the SMO, the *Montgomery Improvement Association*. (Later, in 1957, in Atlanta, the movement would form the SMO, the *Southern Christian Leadership Conference*, also with King at the helm.)

It took over a year (December 2, 1955 to December 20, 1956) for the bus boycott to break the legal segregation of public transportation in Montgomery,[167] but Montgomery had mobilized Black constituents. It began to seem more dangerous not to press one's case, than to press one's case and win.

By 1960, younger activists, in the form of the Student Nonviolent Coordinating Committee (SNCC), began to initiate their own direct actions.[168] Students planned and executed actions, like the lunch counter sit-ins and the Freedom Rides (1961), often without the prior knowledge or approval of older organizers in groups like the SCLC. Younger activists were influenced by other movements, including African nationalist thinkers like Franz Fanon,[169] and some began to postulate a more radical, separatist direction.[170] The assassination of the Rev. Dr. Martin Luther King, Jr. had a devastating impact on the liberal, integrationist branch of the movement, and gave additional impetus to the more radical ideologies of separatism and self-empowerment.

New Left

The late 1950s and early 1960s saw the rise of the New Left, and one of the key early sites was the University of California, Berkeley. University administrations and faculty operated under the common law assumption of "in loco parentis"[171] and as part of their parental oversight, often forbid student political involvement in activism. At Berkeley, students began to demand that policies prohibiting student political speech and activities on campus be changed.[172] In 1957, members of Berkeley's student government founded an organization they named *Towards an Active Student Community* (TASC).[173] With the Civil Rights movement well under way, the first issue TASC tackled was racial discrimination at Berkeley. At the time, racial discrimination was written into the national charters of many sororities and fraternities, and commonplace in university housing and employment. TASC also campaigned against the House Un-American Activities Committee, nuclear testing, involuntary ROTC training, and South African apartheid.[174]

Also beginning in the late 1950s, TASC ran candidates for student government (SLATE)[175] as a means of educating other students about political issues beyond the campus.[176] SLATE ran political education programs, published its own paper, fought against discriminatory hiring and wages, and demanded desegregated university housing. SLATE also began to demand that students be permitted to address national political issues while on the university campus, including: African American civil rights, the death penalty, and educational reform.[177]

44

Similar groups spread to other universities and colleges. In 1960, students protesting a House Un-American Activities Committee hearing in San Francisco were washed down the hall, and down the steps of City Hall, by police wielding fire hoses.[178] Protestors returned en masse the next day.

Also by the early 1960s, administration disenfranchised graduate students for SLATE membership and political activism, and Berkeley's campus saw the rise of the *Free Speech Movement* (FSM), forwarded by students who had volunteered during the Civil Rights Movement's *Freedom Summer* voter's registration campaign.[179] During the Fall 1964 semester, FSM was the first of the 1960s student movements to make headlines all over the world. Lasting a little over two months, it ended with the arrest of 773 persons for occupying the administration building, the removal of the campus administration, and a vast enlargement of student rights to use the University campus for political activity and debate.[180]

Peace/Anti-War Movements

The mid-to late-sixties also saw the rise of united student activism against the war on campuses across the country. The first protests against the war in Vietnam began, in 1963, as U.S. involvement there increased.[181] The U.S. deployed land troops there after reports that two U.S. destroyers were attacked in the Gulf of Tonkin in 1964. Facing involuntary conscription, young activists, already politically savvy from other movements, questioned U.S. involvement and protested the war.

However, it was not until 1965 that the anti-war movement began to hit its stride.[182] Johnson's "massive . . . military intervention" and "sustained bombing of North Vietnam" provided the catalyst for movement mobilization.[183] Student "teach-ins" were held across the country.[184] Students for a Democratic Society (SDS) organized a march on Washington that drew about 20,000 supporters.[185]

Like other, especially younger, movements, the anti-war movement was "less a unified army than a rich mix of political notions and visions."[186] The anti-war movement used strategies like, "demonstrations, grassroots organizing, congressional lobbying, electoral challenges, civil disobedience, draft resistance [including "national draft card turn-ins"], self-immolations, [and] political violence."[187]

Between 1965 and 1967, students from the FSM and from *Students for a Democratic Society* (SDS) participated in direct actions against the Army Induction Center in Oakland, California. By 1967, there was "a national organization of draft resisters."[188] By the mid- to late-sixties draft evaders and deserters were relocating in large numbers to Canada. Anti-war activists raided draft boards, destroyed records, demonstrated against chemical and munitions manufacturers, most especially Dow, and ran into clashes with police. At Columbia, student anti-war protestors occupied university administration offices.

At the 1968 Democratic National Convention in Chicago, Mayor Daly ordered his troops to brutalize protestors.[189] Despite that, by 1968, with both footage of brutality against student protestors and a ceaseless stream of pictures of the devastation of war on the nightly news, public opinion had shifted against the war.

Both the increasing brutality against student protestors, largely White, and the ceaseless images of the devastation of the war on the nightly news, shifted public opinion.[190] "In April 1967, more than 300,000 people demonstrated against the war in New York. Six months later, 50,000 surrounded the Pentagon, sparking nearly 700 arrests. By 1968, the March on Washington drew half a million."[191]

The 1970 Mi Lai massacre and the subsequent invasion of Cambodia was immediately followed by the attack of the Ohio National Guard on student protestors at Kent State, killing four and wounding sixteen, and Mississippi police at Jackson State, killing two and wounding twelve. These military actions against the nation's youth brought renewed student protests, shutting down campuses in a nationwide strike.[192] It came to place where even "GIs protested the war."[193] Another march on Washington in 1971 brought another 500,000 demonstrators, leading to 12,000 arrests.[194] In 1971, the publication of the Pentagon Papers by the *New York Times* demonstrated that, even as he had promised de-escalation, the war had been intentionally escalated by Johnson. This information further reduced government credibility.[195] Given the dramatic and overwhelming demand for an end to the war, by January 1973, Nixon had little choice but to announce the end of the war.[196]

Second-Wave Women's Rights Activism

As with other movements, between the waves (when activism is out of the public eye), limited numbers of activists and SMOs, continued to labor for the cause. In 1923, on the occasion of the 75th anniversary of the first Women's Rights Convention (held in Seneca Falls, NY), Alice Paul, whose militant tactics (gleaned from the British suffrage movement), were largely responsible for passage of the 19th Amendment, wrote – and read – the text of the Equal Rights Amendment (ERA)[197] from the steps of the Presbyterian Church, at 23 Cayuga Street, in Seneca Fall. Paul then had it submitted to every session of Congress from 1923 until it's passage in 1972. *(Although the ERA passed through Congress in 1972, the ERA failed to win ratification before the Congressional deadline of June 30, 1982. So it did not become law. We do not have an Equal Rights Amendment to the Constitution.)*

So, after securing the vote, Paul continued to labor for women's rights, from 1920, through the 1960s and on, until her death in 1977. Handfuls of other first-wave feminists continued to labor as well, including Jeanette Rankin, and the other members of Paul's, *National Woman's Party* (NWP).

In 1963, Betty Friedan's, *The Feminine Mystique*, started a firestorm of self-recognition among many (mostly) White, (mostly) middle-class, (mostly) married women. It pointed out the "problem that has no name" – the vague, empty, discontent of adult (often educated) women trapped in a domestic world of home and childcare, without meaningful outside work, adult interaction, or sufficient mental stimulation. She went on to delineate the shifts in the cultural and media representations of women – before, during, and after World War II – demonstrating the intentionality of the ways women were pushed out of the home for the war effort, and back into the home – into the seclusion of the Domestic Sphere – to free up jobs for returning male veteran's, at war's end.

Her readers – suffering "the problem that has no name," dissatisfied with their mandated social confinement to the roles of homemaker, wife, and mother – passed her book hand-to-hand at kitchen table coffee klatches and over suburban fences, generating a sense of consciousness among the gender-disempowered daughters of race and class privilege. As that consciousness grew, liberal feminists began to demand female inclusion in the male public domain – pressing out of the home and into colleges, and (with those degrees) into meaningful employ.

It is not just cliché to say that the 1960s, fraught as they were by Cold War fear, and shattered by recurring assassinations, were turbulent. At their beginning, confidence in the U.S. government ran high. By their end, the babies born in the post-war boom had come of age disaffected with that same government. They had grown up in a land of plenty – but without a sense of safety – running for shelter to the sound of air raid sirens, sure they wouldn't live till 30 because of atomic and nuclear weapons. The newness of the nuclear age created an air of fatalism that was hard to escape. From their school desks they heard that political leader after political leader had fallen to the inexplicability of an assassin's bullets. On the nightly news, the U.S. military involvement in Vietnam invaded their homes, and they watched, at personal risk. Military service was involuntary – by conscription, not choice – and those still at home watched, as those that preceded them, came home broken in body, broken in mind, or broken and in body bags. And even as the legacy of entrenched racism lit the night skies of U.S. cities orange with flame, the children of race and class privilege – when they exercised the social movement repertoire they considered to be their democratic birthright – were also met with police and state-sponsored violence.

Like the first-wave women's rights activists, who cut their teeth in the abolition movement, the women of that younger cohort of Baby Boomers – who became the radicals of the second-wave of women's rights activists – frequently did so after working in the other social movements of the time. Like the first-wave, they came to a consciousness of their own subordinate position in juxtaposition to males within the other movements of their day. This younger cohort of second-wave activists expected equality *within* the social justice movements. They expected their labor, and their intellectual contributions, to be valued and received, but instead experienced inequality for their sex – even as they fought for the equality of others: men and boys of all colors being drafted and sent into a seemingly senseless war, men of color facing the extremes of racism but not cognizant of the gendered experience of women of color at the intersections of sexism and racism, gay men not cognizant of the gendered experience of lesbian women at the intersections of heterosexism/homophobia and sexism, and often, racism. . . . They found themselves valued only for their sexual and culinary, not their strategic and leadership, contributions. In 1964, Stokley Carmichael (who later changed his name to Kwame Ture) is reported to have said, "the only position for women in SNCC [*the Student Nonviolent Coordinating Committee*] is prone."[198]

This experience of being demeaned *within* liberation movements gave them a more radical edge than their mothers, the housewives reading Friedan. While Friedan and NOW pressed for women's inclusion in the status quo of the "establishment" (a more "liberal" agenda), their daughters (female activists coming out of the New Left, anti-war, and civil rights movements) were in ideological opposition to "the establishment" *before* they came to feminist consciousness, and sought –not rights and inclusion – but the more radical "liberation."

Their feminism was markedly more radical than that of their mothers. They demanded more than entrance to education and the professions. They demanded more than equal pay for equal work. They demanded an end to the sexual division of labor (both outside – and inside – the home), and an end to the sexual double standard (the double standard for male and female sexual expression, autonomy, and freedom from harm). They expected to be received on an equal footing with males in all situations: political, economic, liberation movement, social, and interpersonal. They developed a critique of power within the personal.

Lesbianism became central within the second-wave of women's activism. While women-whose-primary-relational-connections-are-with-other-women *(women-identified women and/ or lesbians[199])* have been central in the multiple waves of women's rights activism (in part, because – before contraception was widely available – not being romantically/relationally-involved with men kept these women more free from the time-consuming burdens of childbearing and childrearing that (often still) isolate women in the home and pull them out of movement work), they were central even in groups that meant to exclude them (like the *National Organization of Women* (NOW), in which, in 1969, Betty Friedan worried aloud that "The Lavender Menace" would damage the movement in the public eye). But it was within the radical wing of the second wave movement that lesbianism became an ideology and the bedroom a particularly political place.

Whatever portion of liberationist women would have identified as same-sex attracted (primarily sexually/affectionally-oriented to other women), women who had up until that time accepted the society's compulsory heterosexuality, began – as part of their critique of power within the sexual – to practice political lesbianism – sleeping with other women rather than sleeping with men as a way to live out their politics.[200]

At the same time, women who *were already* same-sex attracted demanded recognition of the double jeopardy (woman and lesbian) and intricacies of working out a life, at the intersection of gender and sexual orientation.

While liberationist women of color (some of them heterosexual and some of them lesbian-identified), fueled a vital recognition of the double jeopardy of life at the intersection of gender and race/ethnicity,[201] and/or of the triple jeopardy of life at the intersection of gender, race/ethnicity, and sexual orientation.[202] They critiqued the exclusionary perspectives of White privilege[203] (in both the liberal and the radical branches of second-wave women's activism), delineated their own lived experiences and perspectives as women of color, and demanded the inclusion of race and class in the growing political analysis of women's statuses,[204] affirming that oppressions interlocked and could neither be teased apart nor ranked.[205]

Second-wave feminists of all races and classes created multiple social movement organizations meant to function as alternatives to establishment facilities that failed to meet their needs. The women's self-care movement encouraged women to take their own health, especially in the fields of gynecology and obstetrics, into their own hands.[206] Second-wave feminists demanded that female rape victims be recognized as such,[207] and be treated by female staff whenever and wherever possible, including: female doctors, female police officers, and female rape counselors.[208] They formed and opened grassroots rape crisis centers, domestic violence shelters, and telephone emergency hotlines.[209] They also undertook the project of recovering women's history and demanded women's inclusion in school curriculum, leading to the creation of women's studies programs and women's history month.[210]

Free Love and Beyond: Sexual Freedom Movements

Concurrent with the 18th century shifts to more democratic forms of government and the rise of social movements, there was an ongoing shift from subsistence economies based on agriculture to early capitalist, and then industrializing, economies based on wage-labor. This shift changed the historic ground of sexuality, weakening its ties to marriage as a means of economic survival.[211] Increasingly, urban and industrial economies allowed for individual economic autonomy from the family unit. By the late nineteenth and early twentieth centuries, this economic autonomy could even extend to women. As women became less entirely dependent on marriage for economic subsistence, marriage was loosened from its moorings to economics, and romantic "love" became the primary grounds for marriage.[212] Youth began to date unchaperoned, and women and men (not quite content with life inside small rural communities) moved from the farms to the cities.[213] These economic and population shifts contributed to the advent of sexual freedom movements.

An ideology of sexual freedom developed (from Mary Wollstonecraft to Victoria Woodhull, from the Free Love to the hygiene and birth control movements, from the bohemians to the hippies). In the 1960s, birth control information and devices were decriminalized and reliable birth control methods became widely available. These factors (an ideology of sexual freedom, population shifts from rural to urban spaces, the industrialization of the economy, another shift from religion to science (with the rise of sexology and psychology), and the creation and dissemination of *The* (Birth Control) *Pill*, liberated sex and sexuality from its immediate connection to pregnancy (procreation), and women became (potentially) economically self-sustainable units.

The confluence of these factors allowed the "sexual revolution" of the mid-twentieth century. The mainstream, heterosexual population moved from a *sex-in-marriage-only* model to an increasing public approval of *sex* (and even childbirth) *outside of marriage*, with cohabitation before, or even, instead of, marriage.

This same unmooring of marriage from economics, and of the individual from the family and community unit, allowed for same-sex, sexual activity to move from Religion's "sin" and "unnatural" to

54

Psychology's "inversion" and "natural to some." Also important to gay and lesbian movements was the effect of two world wars that brought gay men and lesbians together from all over the country, and all over the world, in port cities – facilitating an increase in (sometimes racially segregated)[214] urban meeting spaces for gay men[215] and urban social – and women's movement spaces – for lesbians.[216]

U.S. Lesbian and Gay Movements

Most historians date the rise of the LGBTQ movement to the riot at the Stonewall Inn in Greenwich Village in June of 1969. However, multiple factors important to this discussion led up to Stonewall – including prior resistance at Compton's Cafeteria in San Francisco (1966).[217]

Evidence of same-sex sexual behavior exists in many cultures, locations, and times. Within the Western discourse, until the end of the 19th century, same-sex sexual behavior was framed as "perversion" and "sin," but not as an identity.

With the rise of psychology and sexology, theorists like Richard von Krafft-Ebing (1886), Havelock Ellis (1901, 1915), and Sigmund Freud (1920) began to define sexuality within a medical model, and hypothesized same-sex sexual desire as a disorder ("immature" and "maladjusted") juxtaposed against a norm of "mature" and "adjusted" heterosexuality.[218]

Much of the discrimination against homosexuals – *as homosexuals* – as particular kinds of persons – dates from their theories. Those with same-sex desires came to be seen as a certain category of (disordered) persons that could be grouped together. The majority of anti-gay laws were enacted – not in the 18th or 19th Centuries – but in the early- to mid-20th century – between 1930 and 1950,[219] and these laws resulted in persecutions (police harassment, police entrapment, public exposure after arrest, imprisonment) so that – as individuals and as a group – homosexuals were then "systematically denied . . . [their] right to free assembly, to patronize public accommodations together, to free speech, to a free press, [and] to a form of [consensual] intimacy of their own choosing."[220]

This flurry of anti-homosexual law creation is the effect of psychological labeling, and may also be attributable to fears about masculinity brought up by the changes in gender roles of the Great Depression[221] and as backlash against the first-wave of women's rights activism.[222]

Some of this backlash also played out in morals crusades, by groups like the Catholic Legion of Decency, who pressed for the passage of the Hays Code, which barred gay and lesbian themes and characters from Hollywood film, and imposed public censorship on the Broadway stage.[223]

Nevertheless, psychological labeling had the effect of facilitating homosexual identity formation, so that gays and lesbians increasingly began to think of themselves – not as individually disordered and ashamed – but as part of a group (and ultimately, a group with rights), and despite the vice codes and police harassment, gay and lesbian gathering places (and social organizations) formed and increased during and after World War II.

In the attempt to prevent homosexuals from enlisting, or being conscripted, into military service, the military imposed "government sanction[ed]" stereotyping,[224] putting recruits through questionnaires and psychiatric tests designed to eliminate gays and lesbians. These had the unintended effect of causing young men and women to evaluate the possibilities.

Across the country, from the early 1900s, through into the 1970s, gays and lesbians did time in (or experienced electric shock and lobotomies in) prisons and mental hospitals as incurable sexual deviants – for nothing more than being caught having (*or entrapped by undercover police into suggesting*) consensual adult-to-adult sex, or for being suspected by family of being same-sex oriented.[225] Outside of the military, a majority of states empowered police to mandate psychiatric evaluations for anyone "convicted of . . . sodomy" or "suspected of being sexually "deviant.""[226] Often, these laws then allowed for "indefinite" psychiatric commitment for those so diagnosed. Long-term involuntary commitment to mental hospitals – often at the request of family and sometimes for life – was a real possibility, with or without police intrusion.[227] Release was only to be had, upon "cure," which "prison doctors soon" saw as "impossible."[228]

In 1953, President Eisenhower "banned homosexuals from government employment, civilian as well as military," and "required companies with government contracts to ferret out and fire their gay employees [by] executive order."[229] Under McCarthyism, "the U.S. State Department fired more homosexuals than communists."[230] And because homosexuals were considered psychopathic, in 1952 Congress closed the doors of immigration to homosexuals.[231]

Legislation was passed against gay patronage of restaurants and bars.[232] Between the 1930s and 1970, gay bars across the country served as the tough-on-vice platform of many politicians and were the sites of continual police harassment. With nowhere else to meet other gays or lesbians (either for community, friendship, or for lovers or partners), gay patrons faced an "unimaginable" level of police harassment, living with the constant threat of exposure via arrest and newspaper coverage.[233] In the late 1940s, New York City police were making (and publicizing) about 3000 arrests per year. And in Philadelphia, in 1950, the "morals squad" made about 2400 per year.[234] Stonewall was the turning back of these 20th century intrusions into gay lives and gathering spaces.

Homophile Movement

In the U.S., resistance to the increased oppression of the early 20th century began almost at once. In the 1920s, Henry Gerber began to organize.[235] In 1924, he founded *The Society for Human Rights* and published *Friendship and Freedom*. He was stopped in 1925 when police raided his Chicago home office and files, arrested him, and three other Society members, and jailed them for three days.[236] Charges were not filed, but Gerber lost his postal job and was tried multiple times.[237]

In 1951, despite McCarthyism, the Mattachine Society was formed and became "the first national gay rights group" to succeed in getting off the ground. Given the climate, it had to "repeatedly . . . reassure its anxious members that the police would not seize its membership list."[238]

Early homophile publications suffered under postal "obscenity laws," making it difficult to organize.[239] "The U.S. Post Office banned [the Mattachine] newspaper [*One*] from the mails in 1954," and "in some cities the police shut down newsstands that dared to carry it."[240]

One of the founders of Mattachine, Harry Hay, was one of the first to theorize homosexuals as a legitimate "minority" group.[241] Under Hay, Mattachine ran discussion groups, published a magazine, organized against entrapment, and leafleted gay sites.[242] They also formulated "a comprehensive vision of social and political change" and were willing "to challenge anti-homosexual attacks even in the midst of McCarthyism."[243] Hay drew on Communist models for inspiration in organizing and effecting social change.[244] In its founding statement . . . Mattachine pledged . . ."to assist 'our people who are victimized daily as a result of our oppression'."[245] Hay left Mattachine when the majority desired a social, rather than a political, emphasis.[246]

Also in 1951, using the pseudonym Daniel Webster Cory, Edward Sagarin also argued that "homosexuals were an oppressed minority."[247] Corey's book "offered the only publicly available presentation of gay life by a homosexual writer."[248] Corey went on to argue, "that homosexuals constituted a minority group that deserved its rights like any other."[249] This ground of collective identity formation permitted individuals to organize and mobilize.[250] Rupp writes, "What was new under the postwar sun was the formation of lasting [gay] organizations."[251] Along with Cold War McCarthyism, the tenor of the times was affected by the fact that World War II had been fought "against Nazi racism" and that the U.S. played a leading role in developing the U.N. *Universal Declaration of Human Rights*.[252] Along with self-affirmation, homophile activists "sought "allies among . . . professionals who had the credibility to speak on homosexuality."[253] This tactic (along with more confrontational tactics like poster displays and gay kissing ["Hug a Homosexual] booths at conferences) promoted the research that helped to get homosexuality removed, in 1973, from the American Psychological Association's DSM-III (*Diagnostic and Statistical Manual*) list of psychiatric disorders.[254]

Ultimately, the homophile movement was more accommodationist than the gay liberation movement it preceded. Homophile organizations are remembered for arguing the social movement claim that, except in sexual object choice, homosexuals are no different than other Americans. However, demands that become "liberal" or "accommodationist" are often quite radical at their outset: "It is easy enough to . . . fault . . . the homophile movement for its accommodationist tactics, but it is important to remember just how much it meant that members felt no need to apologize for being gay or lesbian,"[255] and a good six years before the Stonewall Resistance, homophile organizations were becoming more militant.[256]

In San Francisco, in 1962, "the proprietors and employees of several of the city's gay bars formed the Tavern Guild to fight police harassment."[257] And when "the homophile groups of New York, Philadelphia, and Washington joined together in 1963 to form a coalition known as ECHO (*East Coast Homophile Organizations*), forces within and without . . . began to veer away from the politics of assimilation and respectability."[258]

On July 4th, 1965, ECHO organized the first of five Independence Day protests (*Annual Reminders*) in front of Philadelphia's

Independence Hall, "as a reminder that the Declaration of Independence had not brought freedom to all."[259] These protests "drew national media attention and gave visibility to gays and lesbians."[260] Before Stonewall, gay and transgender customers rioted in response to police harassment at Compton's Cafeteria in San Francisco (1966), and police raids at *The Black Cat Tavern* in Los Angeles (1967) also "provoked a demonstration on Sunset Boulevard,"[261] and the formation of a paper which became *The Advocate*. [262]

Resistance & Pride

In 1969, the series of riots known as the Stonewall Uprising "marked the public emergence of a long-repressed, covert urban subculture."[263] Within days of the riots at, and around, the Stonewall, the community began to organize and the New York *Gay Liberation Front* was formed in a split from the New York *Mattachine Society*. The Gay Liberation Front "recruited" from "the New Left and the women's movement," and "borrowed . . . confrontational tactics from these movements."[264]

In 1970, the *Homophile Action League* cancelled its planned demonstration (the "*Annual Reminder*" that lesbians and gays didn't have civil rights – held for five years – on July 4th – at Independence Hall, from 1965 through 1969), to work instead on the *Christopher Street Liberation Day* parade (June 28, 1970),[265] organizing in New York City to "commemorating Stonewall" one year before,[266] Since that first parade (as both demonstrations making demands and celebrations of personal pride) annual LGBTQ *Pride* parades have sprung up across the country, and around the globe.

Gay Social Movement Organizations

The sudden, increased militance of the gay liberation movement was youth-driven and may, in part, be linked to the "disaffection from American society" common among youth movements.[267] Young militants, with their consciousness raised by the Civil Rights, New Left, Anti-War, and fledgling Women's Rights movements, responded to police harassment of their public meeting places (bars), public shaming after entrapment and arrest, and unfavorable articles and news reports,[268] with marches and demonstrations. Gay Liberation groups disrupted political, medical, and psychiatric conventions, used "confrontational tactics," and intentionally drew media attention by their "flamboyant behavior." This media attention swelled the ranks of the newly-mobilized.[269] Thousands of independent, local, gay social movement organizations sprang up around the country.[270] *Gay Liberation Fronts* (GLFs), *Gay Activist Alliances* (GAAs), student *Homophile Leagues*, and lesbian feminist groups sprang up on college campuses and in major cities.[271] They "adopted militant strategies and proudly asserted their right to define their own sexualities," and by 1973, there were "more than eight hundred" across the country.[272] The *GLF* agenda included "oppos[ing] consumer culture, militarism, racism, and sexism,"[273] and the *GAA* "lobbied" for "fair employment and housing legislation," the "repeal" of "sodomy and solicitation" laws, and for "banning" "police entrapment and harassment."[274]

However, while early groups, like the *Gay Liberation Front* (GLF) and the *Gay Activist Alliance* (GAA) were influential, they were also short lived.[275]

Yet, a number of still-existent national organizations began relatively early. In 1973, the *Lambda Legal Defense and Education Fund* (Lambda) was founded, modeled after the NAACP *(National Association for the Advancement of Colored People) Defense and Education Fund*.[276] Through a network of headquarters and lawyers, Lambda fights to change the legal landscape. Its arenas have included: the repeal of sodomy laws,[277] housing and employment discrimination, AIDS discrimination, second parent adoption and visitation, child custody, hospital visitation, immigration restrictions, gay straight alliances, school bullying, hate crimes, dishonorable military discharges, inheritance and pension rights, and relationship recognition (domestic partnership/reciprocal beneficiary/civil unions/ and ultimately, civil marriage).[278]

The *National Gay & Lesbian Task Force* (NGLFT) was founded in 1973 as a lobbying organization to promote pro-LGBTQ, and oppose anti-LGBTQ, legislation.[279] The *NGLTF* website reports,

> The Task Force played a critical role in the campaign to eliminate the sickness classification of homosexuality. It worked to lift the prohibition on federal civil service employment. . . . It strove in the 1970's to make the Democratic Party responsive to the gay community. It took the lead in the 1980's in national organizing against homophobic violence. As AIDS began to devastate gay male communities, the Task Force shaped the first

63

serious efforts in Washington to address the epidemic. It was a founding member of the Military Freedom Project, which prepared the ground for the gays-in-the-military debate of 1993."[280]

The *Human Rights Campaign* (HRC) was founded in 1980 to raise money to support pro-LGBTQ candidates for congress. *HRC* lobbies on Capitol Hill. It worked to elect Bill Clinton to the presidency, and unsuccessfully fought against the federal Defense of Marriage Act (DOMA) and for the Employment Non-Discrimination Act (ENDA). It has lobbied for national gay and transgender-inclusive hate crimes legislation. *HRC* continues to raise funds for pro-gay candidates, lobbies for gay marriage, and monitors corporations for the LGBTQ-inclusive policies.[281]

Modeled after the *B'nai B'rith Anti-Defamation League* (Chauncey 2004:32), the *Gay and Lesbian Alliance Against Defamation* (GLAAD) was founded in 1985 "to protest the New York Post's . . . AIDS coverage."[282] *GLAAD* monitors representations of LGBTQ people in the media. *GLAAD's* activism has resulted in the use of the word "gay" in the press, newspaper inclusion of "same-sex union announcements," and media attention to hate crimes (including Matthew Shepard, Brandon Teena, and Gwen Araujo) and to the victims of 9-11, known to be gay, whose families did not receive equal treatment.

Sexual Liberation

The gay liberation movement was a sexual freedom movement that "publicly . . . celebrat[ed] . . . homosexual difference."[283] However, gay liberation also benefited from changes occurring across the country for heterosexuals, like the disconnection of heterosexual sex from reproduction and marriage. "The mass decision to come out was encouraged by the sexual revolution."[284] In "the mid-1960s through the 1970s," largely because of shifts in both legal and reliable birth control, there was "an epochal shift" throughout the Western world, in the "sexual behavior and norms . . . [that had] limited sex to marriage."[285] Prohibitions on all non-marital, non-reproductive sex were lifted as "a new moral code . . . linked sex to love and common consent" took their place.[286] In the new social configuration, "many . . . insisted on frankness in sexual matters," and this "encouraged" lesbians and gay men to become open about their sexual orientation.[287]

Anti-Gay Backlash

The "coming out" impetus, for as much as it empowered gay lives and activism, "frightened many . . . outsiders" and "made gay freedom a primary target" of conservatives seeking to re-impose "traditional family values."[288] In 1977, Anita Bryant began her *Save Our Children* campaign in Dade Country, Florida, intent on *defeating an anti-discrimination* bill. In her rhetoric, she "depended heavily on . . . the still powerful postwar images of homosexuals as child molesters."[289] Her "victory" inspired other conservative groups, "and in the next three years, gay rights laws were struck down in more than half a dozen bitterly fought referenda."[290]

Jerry Falwell founded the political *Moral Majority*, and Pat Robertson founded the candidate-evaluating *Christian Coalition*, to mobilize a conservative Christian constituency to "take back" the country politically. Robertson (and others, like Paul and Jan Crouch and Jim and Tammy Bakker) organized networks of Christian broadcasters, thus creating a national platform with which to campaign against reproductive and gay rights under the banner of "family values."[291] Also, from the perspective of the AIDS crisis that broke during "the first year of his administration," the election of Ronald Reagan, on the back of the politically mobilized conservative evangelical vote, "could not have come at a worse time."[292]

Plague

News of gay men dying of *pneumocystis carinii pneumonia* (PCP) and a "gay cancer," *Kaposi's sarcoma* (KS) – followed by news of a "gay-related immune deficiency" (GRID) – broke in 1981. The connection of gay men, and gay male sexual practices, with hysteria about an infection feared to endanger all, fueled a backlash that manifested in both social discrimination and government inaction. Gay men, "guilty" of lurid sex, were juxtaposed with the "innocent:" those infected through transfusion and 'positive' babies born to drug-addicted mothers. "Fear of contagion prompted a new wave of discrimination against gay people in medical care, housing, and employment [as] heterosexuals became afraid to use the same phones or water fountains [and] protests by parents forced schools to expel children with AIDS."[293]

Within the homosexual community, "AIDS . . . led to an unprecedented mobilization of gay men and an equally unprecedented" interaction between gay men and lesbians, who "played leading roles in the response to AIDS."[294] Rapid mobilization was enabled by the number of SMOs already in place because of the gay liberation movement.[295]

By 1982, "gay male and lesbian activists formed the *Gay Men's Health Crisis* (GMHC) in New York City and the *Kaposi's Sarcoma Research and Education Foundation* in San Francisco, which two years later became the *San Francisco AIDS Foundation*."[296] However, in the midst of the epidemic, AIDS activist organizations frequently became AIDS service organizations, disseminating safe sex and medical information and tending to the dying. Other organizations were necessary to dramatize the severity of the crisis, and raise mainstream consciousness, through political confrontation and art.[297]

In 1985, The *NAMES Project AIDS Memorial Quilt* began as "community artwork to commemorate the lives of those who had died." [298] In 1987, when it was laid out on the National Mall in Washington, D.C. "during the *March on Washington for Lesbian and Gay Rights*" it contained 1,920 panels. One year later, it contained 8,000. By 2003, it contained 44,000 panels, "representing 83,000 names (19% of all AIDS deaths in the United States at that time)."[299]

Formed in 1987, *ACT UP* "focused on . . . the FDA and drug companies" demanding that they "streamline clinical trials."[300] They "pressure[d] governmental officials and community leaders to respond" demanding "more effective and accessible treatment options."[301] They made use of direct action and art to dramatize the fact that the government was not responding while gay men were dying almost faster than they could be buried. Ministers of the only gay denomination, the *Universal Fellowship of Metropolitan Community Churches (UFMCC)*, report officiating multiple funerals a day in New York and California at the height of the crisis. [302]

In 1988, *Gran Fury* took art to the streets to "inform a broad public" and "render complex issues understandable" through creating a "visual form" for the AIDS statistics."[303] In 1989, the *Visual AIDS Artist's Caucus* "created the *Red Ribbon Project* . . . as a symbol of commitment to people with AIDS and to the AIDS-struggle. Sponsored by the group *Broadway Cares/Equity Fights AIDS*, the *Red Ribbon* debuted at the televised 1991 Tony Awards."[304]

These projects succeeded at raising mainstream consciousness about the realities of the AIDS crisis within the gay community. They disseminated information, making it clear that HIV is not spread through non-sexual social contact, thus de-demonizing gay men as vectors of infection. And they motivated medical and governmental institutions to supply research and treatments. Even though treatments for HIV have abated the intensity of the crisis, at this writing AIDS activism faces new challenges as the U.S. congress debates "reforms" in AIDS funding that will cut monies to the regional populations most affected by new and standing U.S. cases, and as AIDS continues to have a profound impact upon other nations, especially Asia and Sub-Saharan Africa.

Queer Nation was founded in 1990, in New York City, to address the increasing incidence of anti-queer violence through visibility and direct action urging queers to "bash back." In 1992, *Lesbian Avengers* was founded to increase lesbian visibility in the movement, through street theater and annual *Dyke Marches*, as alternatives to the often-male-dominated *Gay Pride* parades and their cooptation by corporate interests. Increasingly in the 1990s, younger activists came to use the word "queer" in juxtaposition to "gay and lesbian," which they increasingly saw as assimilationist and exclusionary of multiple portions of sexual minority communities.

Cultural/Coming Out Movement

The gay/lesbian/bisexual/transgender and/or queer movements (LGBTQ) have not been restricted to the realm of the political. The cultural segment of the LGBTQ movement begins before Stonewall. Like second-wave feminism, and other movements that have connected the personal with the political, gay social movements have been intricately connected with the cultural. Even though Broadway and Hollywood were restricted in their ability to address LGBTQ themes and protagonists, from the early 20th century some gay novelists were able to tackle gay and lesbian lives in their work.[305]

The rise of the pulp novel, which dates for gay men from the 1940s,[306] and dates for lesbians from the 1950s,[307] permitted a space in which gay authors could sometimes construct lives and relationships that mirrored gay realities rather than canned morality tales.[308]

Homophile organizations had founded newsletters and magazines, but the 1970s gay liberation/lesbian feminist movements made use of "free press" publishing tactics common in the anti-war, New Left, and civil rights movements. Alternative bookstores, free newspapers, and movement publishing houses were founded across the country.

In the more metropolitan areas, the early 1970s brought new networks of gay and gay-friendly religious spaces, and the 1980s and 1990s saw the creation of LGBTQ community centers offering a wide range of community services. These movements reduced the dependence of gay culture on gay bars.

With the 1990s rise of the Internet, online communities have sprung up and international gay news is rapidly disseminated. Along with the possibilities of online dating and friendship acquisition, internet groups, listserves, and online calendars provide opportunities for LGBTQ individuals to host local social events that reduce isolation in less-urban areas. The online presence of local and national LGBTQ SMOs, and information sharing, is having a revolutionary effect on LGBTQ consciousness, both within the United States and globally.[309]

Interestingly, the gay movement has "continued to thrive" even as other movements have waned. At least one scholar credits this survival to "the new definition that post-Stonewall activists gave to "coming out" – which "doubled both as ends and [as] means."[310] While some earlier homophile leaders, like Barbara Gittings and Frank Kameny, bravely gave a public face to the movement themselves, in general, homophile thought "only rarely" counseled "lesbians and homosexuals at large" to come out, concentrating more on creating covert social community. Separate from, and in addition to, mass mobilization efforts, gay SMOs encouraged coming out as daily resistance to oppression.[311] Gay Liberationists "recast coming out as a profoundly political act" with "enormous personal benefits."[312] *HRC* forwarded the effort with its annual *National Coming Out Day* impetus.

Coming out became a rejection of internalized homophobia, self-affirmation, "pride" in being gay, "the fusion of the personal and the political," "cathartic," "exhilaration and anger," and a successful "key strategy" for movement building.[313] This coming out strategy "propelled" rank-and-file gays and lesbians into "movement activity," because in crossing that "dividing line" and "relinquish[ing] invisibility," lesbians and gays became invested.

Coming out renders movement adherents more visible and, therefore, more "vulnerable to attack." It creates "an army of permanent enlistees," who find it difficult to "fade back" into heterosexual privilege.[314] And coming out swells the ranks in another way. Individuals who are boldly gay serve as a "magnet[s]" to those who are still in the closet.[315] The more people there are that are "out," the more closeted individuals know *how* to find a path into the community.

The coming out strategy also affects heterosexuals. "The mass movement to come out succeeded in humanizing lesbians and gay men for many outsiders, making the demonization of homosexuality less persuasive and less acceptable, and rallying many heterosexuals to support the rights of people they now realized were not alien pariahs but often among those they most loved and respected."[316]

Television slowly began to take on gay themes and characters in the 1970s. Norman Lear spearheaded the issue twice on *All in the Family* and Billy Crystal played a gay character on *Soap*. However, it was not until Ellen DeGeneres came out, along with her character, in 1997, that television really began (despite the cancellation of her show) to take on central gay characters. In the early 2000s, there was a relative-proliferation of gay-themed shows (*Will and Grace, Queer Eye for the Straight Guy, Queer as Folk, the L-Word*) and the LGBTQ television channel, LOGO.

The gay cultural movement has also grown through important (voluntary and involuntary) celebrity and political "outings." The somber and less-than-voluntary outings of celebrities who died of AIDS, like Rock Hudson and Freddie Mercury of Queen, have been followed by a growing trickle of other celebrities willing to out themselves, including: Ellen, Melissa Etheridge, k.d. lang, Rosie O'Donnell, Chad Everett, Lance Bass, and increasingly more. Gay/transgender relatives of the famous add to the list, including Chaz Bono (female-to-male transgender man, formerly out-as-a lesbian, writer-at-large for The Advocate, spokesperson for *HRC*, and Entertainment Director for *GLAAD*), Candice Gingrich (also connected to *HRC*), and political daughter, Mary Cheney. At this writing, prominent sports figures have begun to publicly out themselves as well, and there is an increasing recognition in corporate America of the value of the LGBTQ dollar as a commercial market and of the importance of LGBTQ employees in the workplace.

The Marriage Equality Movement

Background – The Demand & The Debate

Much of the controversy around the LGBTQ social movement claim for same-sex marriage is based on an ahistorical image of marriage as a universally stable, static, unchanging and unchangeable social institution across geographic and chronologic location. Despite the ahistorical basis of the claim, conservatives, opposing the extension of civil marriage to lesbian and gay couples, argue that marriage has been an essentially unchanged and divinely mandated "union of one man and one woman" over the past four or five millennia. To fend off perceived threats to the heterosexual family – like divorce, blended families, and single- or grandparent-headed households, and same-sex unions[317] – marriage is idealized through the filter of the divided-sphere, nuclear family, circa 1950.[318] Yet, just a brief overview of the history of marriage in Western culture demonstrates that marriage has experienced "enormous variation over time and among cultures" in the ways it "has organized sexual and emotional life, child-rearing, property, kinship, and political alliances."[319] When addressing marriage across time, "many anthropologists are loath to [even] use the term "marriage" at all, since the term's apparently straightforward simplicity hides so much more than it reveals."[320]

Lesbians and gays desired "marriage" (as a longed-for, but remote and unattainable yearning), long before there was a *Marriage Equality* movement.

The project of reclaiming LGBTQ history indicates that there have always been – within any given culture or time – those who were attracted to others of the same sex.

And since same-sex attraction is not just sexual – but like other-sex attraction, also affectional – there is also every reason to believe that there have always been – within any given culture or time (*millennia before gay and lesbian people were labeled by psychologists as inverts or homosexuals, before they came to self-identify as a certain kind of person, before there was democracy-induced identity politics*) – those who fell in love with others of their own sex.

And since it is reasonable to believe that there have always been those who fell in love, within-sex, it is also reasonable to suspect that there have always been same-sex oriented persons who wished to enact their own culture's rituals of family-making with that same-sex other for whom they had feelings. Not only is it reasonable to suspect, there is also anthropological evidence that before there was a movement – before Henry Gerber or Mattachine or the Daughter of Bilitis or Stonewall and the *Gay Activist Alliance*– same-sex couples exchanged tokens, rings, or other articles, and engaged in cultural rituals, as symbols of their commitment to each other.[321]

Some conservative critiques of the LGBTQ demand for marriage make the claim that gay people (perhaps more specifically, gay men) don't really want to be married – but rather, desire only to destroy the foundation of heterosexual marriage.

But the evidence is, that as soon as it became conceivable, gay people begin to make the demand for the right to marry: the gay church movement began to perform "holy unions" and stage annual

Valentine's Day protests at marriage bureaus that denied them the right to apply for a license, more-secular gay and lesbian couples began to enact "commitment ceremonies" and to submit their engagement and wedding announcements to their local papers,[322] and on the 4th of June 1971 (just after Stonewall), the *Gay Activist Alliance* staged a demonstration by taking over the New York City Marriage Bureau offices.[323]

Along with the human desire to enact rites of commitment within sexually-/affectionally-bonded relationships, and to not be excluded from social rites and rituals available to others of similar rank within one's society, an additional impetus to the timing of the rise of the social movement demand for marriage/relationship recognition would be the sudden availability of assisted reproductive technologies, and the impact on LGBTQ people of the massive death of the HIV/AIDS epidemic (and its ongoing pandemic), that demonstrated (even to very young couples) their lack of rights to be there for, and speak up for each other, in death and dying, and in the post-mortem division of their joint property and desired custody arrangements.[324]

Though not physically affected by the AIDS Crisis, lesbians joined gay men in the response to tending and burying the dying and in demanding appropriate medical and government response, and gay male partners (often, but not always, sick themselves) were continually mistreated in hospitals, by mortuary staff, by their dying or deceased partner's families, and in the loss of the life and possessions they had built with their loved one. They came to see how the legal trappings of other-sex committed unions (marriage) worked as a social protection to the establishment of a place in your partner's life – and death. In the face of death, other-sex (heterosexual) married partners were given deference, were in charge of end of life decisions and medical and funeral arrangements, were honored at (not excluded from) memorial services, and were automatic heirs to the couple's marital property in a way that non-spousal family members had no serious legal grounds with which to contest.

As same-sex relationships win legal status, LGBTQ activists in the *marriage equality movement* argue that the attribution of the word "marriage" is essential – that the symbolism and social meaning embedded in the concept of "marriage" is the only "currency" (or "nomenclature") that will secure all of the *rights and benefits* (state, federal, and social) that other-sex couples have and bring about the wide acceptance of same-sex relationships as "equal" with other-sex relationships.[325]

However, there are LGBTQ voices *critical of the marriage claim*, and they argue that opting into marriage as an institution – that simply being subsumed into committed, legally-binding, same-sex, monogamous relationships – will allows the state to continue to deny *rights and benefits* to those who are single, or to those whose affectional lives do not meet the one-partner-at-a-time standard of monogamy. They suggest that we would do better, as a society, if the battle were not for recognition of same-sex relationships that meet a heteronormative standard of commitment, but for changes like a guaranteed living wage, truly accessible and affordable healthcare, and an adequate social safety net for the citizenry at large – that we should shift the burden of social safety from the private sphere of bonded sexual relationships to the public sphere of a compassionate society.[326]

Defining Marriage - Origins

Marriage in one time and place is not comparable with marriage in another, but is rather an institution in a constant state of flux.[327] When one merely looks at the documented "variety of forms of marriage cross-culturally," "the difficulty . . . in defining" it "becomes evident."[328] Differences in that which has been called marriage across culture and era are so vast that "it is difficult, perhaps impossible, to map onto the grid of pre-modern heterosexual relationships [that which] modern speakers understand by "marriage."[329]

When looking at the ancient world, there is "nothing" there that "quite corresponds to the idea of a permanent, exclusive union of social equals, freely chosen by them to fulfill both [of] their emotional needs, and imposing equal obligations of fidelity on both partners."[330]

Marriage appears to have originated in the ownership of – and sexual access to – females, by males, including (but not restricted to) bride sale, bride purchase, and bride kidnapping.[331] One significant purpose of marriage has been to control women's sexuality,[332] in order to regulate economics and inheritance by insuring the legitimacy of male (not female) heirs.[333] Marriage may be viewed as a multi-millennia "political battleground, constantly shifting to suit each culture and class, each era and economy."[334]

Along with controlling women to insure male inheritance, it has also been used to divide labor on grounds of gender,[335] to create between-group alliances and kinship,[336] to control race and class relations,[337] and to create intimacy.[338] In both the ancient, and the pre-modern, European worlds, marriage was only one form of other-sex relationship. Heterosexual relationships had four forms: "marriage," "use," "concubinage," and "romance;"[339] and marriage could be either polygamous or monogamous.[340]

Ancient and Feudal Economics

It was capitalism that has both allowed, and even mandated, present-day individualism. Until industrialization, marriage remained tightly connected to family connections and economics.[341] In ancient and feudal economies, as a matter of survival, marriage was a property arrangement in which the wealth, or labor, of extended family structures was shared with new couples and their offspring.[342] As such, choice of spouse was largely in the hands of parents or other extended family members.[343]

Subsistence was dependent on the collectivity of an extended family, "[T]here [we]re only two ways of making a living: land and labor. . . . If your family ha[d] property, they f[ound] another family with whom to exchange it. Or if" you made your living through labor, they found you "someone else" to "be your business partner, lifelong" to help you farm or earn a family wage.[344] In an economic structure in which survival was based, either on one's family's inherited wealth or on common labor, feudal marriages were arranged by families across acquaintance networks of those in community or household proximity,[345] and "when people marr[ied] for money" they weren't "doing it for venal reasons." They were "doing it not to starve."[346]

Arranged Unions

Social pressures to marry the match one's family chose varied. In some cultures, the consent of the bride's family members was more important than that of the bride[347] (or groom),[348] but in other cultures, arranged marriage has included a bridal right of veto.

In Roman culture, consent was considered to be an important factor.[349]

And though it may often have been violated by social/family pressure, Roman Catholic doctrine has stipulated that the couple that marries each other do so freely and with full consent (they pledge "their "troth").[350] While a priest is counted necessary,[351] it is as a witness to the consecration of "the sacrament" that *they* (the couple) enter into with each other.[352]

Consummation (as a sign of at least male consent) has also been generally considered essential to the final creation of the matrimonial bond, and an unconsummated union may be annulled.

Sexuality was governed by "custom," "kin, slaveowners, masters, church, and state."[353] Love, if it entered the picture at all, was a non-essential afterthought.[354] Only in the literatures of "Augustan Rome, twelfth- and thirteenth-century Europe, and the last two centuries" has "romantic love" been "commonly spoken of."[355] Despite the demand for achieving procreation (and hence, being sexually intimate), the center of any match was its class or economic potential, not it's pleasure/attraction/romance – or it's harm/revulsion – potential. Therefore, emotional interests outside of marriage were commonplace, and often, for men (who were expected to have "needs"), societally-approved, if they did not disrupt the economic stability of the marital union.

From Secular to Religious

Christianity, "for the first thousand years" considered marriage "a secular institution."[356] It was the agreement between contractual parties – the engagement – that was "the tie that binds," with the marriage ceremony itself being little more than an exchange of property.[357] And it was not until 1215 C.E., at the Fourth Lateran Council, that the Roman Church declared the pronouncing of a blessing by a priest, and the publication of banns (so no wedding be done in secret), essential.[358] Before that time, the attendance of clergy at weddings was not only unnecessary, but also rare. After that Council, through the 13th to 16th centuries, the conceptualization of marriage as a religious sacrament grew, and was further defined in 1563 by the Council of Trent (which also condemned concubinage and polygamy and clandestine [secret] marriage, stressing the publication of the banns and the necessity of a priest officiant and two further witnesses).[359]

The "Collapse" of "Traditional" Marriage[360]

Sexuality has been "continually reshaped by the changing nature of the economy, the family, and politics,"[361] yet until industrialization, other-sex marriage had remained tied to family connections and economics,[362] continuing to be a property arrangement in which the wealth or labor of extended family structures was shared with new couples and their offspring.[363] But, with the rise of urbanization and industrialization, the ability to earn an individual wage brought concurrent reductions in familism and of the dependence on extended kinship networks, and the advent of an individualism, that largely disconnected other-sex marriage from economic survival.

The shift was gradual, beginning in the 17th Century, and picking up pace and "transform[ing] dramatically" in the late 19th and early 20th centuries.[364] Between, the mid-1700s and the 1920s this shift "set off changes in every . . . philosophy of marriage," including "what makes sex sacred or even acceptable; what children need to grow up well; how far in or out of their kinship circle . . . people are expected or allowed to marry; what marriage rules are required to keep social order; and how important it is to consult your own heart."[365]

The first and second-wave of women's rights activism wrought "differences in the marital roles."[366] The autonomy, for women, of wage work, the social shift for these autonomous earners from courtship to dating, and the hard won, but increasing, availability of contraception (and contraceptive information) meant that by "1920 . . . every third magazine article [was] saying, "This is the end of marriage as we know it. This is the death of the family.""[367]

Ultimately, it was a shift from the "family-centered, reproductive sexual system" of the 17th Century – to "a romantic," "personal[ly] intimate," middle-class "sexuality," with a reduced birth rate in the 19thCentury – to the "commercialized sexuality" of the 20th and early 21st Centuries, in which marriage and/or sex "are expected to provide" both emotional intimacy and physical pleasure.[368] A final shift was made in the mid-20th Century – when widespread access to birth control information and the availability of new and more reliable birth control methods – rendered women "self-sustaining economic units,"[369] and "the individual," not the family, became "the primary economic unit."[370] This shift moved marriage away from "the control of labor and transmission of property" – changing the way most of us "found our life's main co-worker"[371] – into a romantic institution focused on "happiness and mutual commitment."[372]

While "not everything can be reduced to economics,"[373] "four fundamental changes" have happened "since the nineteenth century" that are "now been embraced" as both a "moral good" and "commonsense"[374]

1. The freedom to marry is considered to be a "right"[375]
2. So, also, is the freedom to end a marriage[376]
3. Arranged marriage went by the wayside for most native-born Americans (partner choice is now "voluntary" and has "come to be seen by the courts and the American people as a fundamental civil right" even across racial lines[377] – and –
4. Mutual consent became "more important than official recognition by the state or church," contributing to cohabitation becoming commonplace.[378]

Yet, even as **other**-sex (heterosexual) marriage decreased as the locus of survival, early 20th Century income tax and social security laws made other-sex marriage the site of federal- and state-allocated economic benefits (including, but not limited to, social security, health and life insurance, and pension beneficiary statuses). These changes established a new mode of heterosexual privilege for other-sex relationships, making civil marriage "a crucial nexus for the allocation of public and private rights and benefits, so that the exclusion of same-sex couples from marriage impose[s] increasingly significant economic and legal consequences."[379]

Thus, while same-sex couples already lived the sting of the social exclusion of their relationships from the rituals of love and commitment, and struggled under the demands of living hidden ("closeted") lives, the political demand for same-sex marriage began, in part, as an effort to be included – as couples – in this new constellation of federal and state couples rights and benefits – especially given the experience of relationship discrimination (exclusion from next-of-kin recognition, exclusion from health care benefits, inheritance discrimination) as partners died in the AIDS crisis.[380]

Evidence of Same-Sex History

As I briefly mentioned earlier, despite cross-location fluctuations in the definition and meanings of marriage, same-sex marriage—even though far from universal in intent or perception—does have cross-cultural antecedents.[381] Anthropologists have documented cross-cultural examples of unions that, if contracted in the U.S. today, "would be considered same-sex marriage,"[382] including; ""female husbands" . . . among the Nuer, Lovedu, Nandi, Yoruba and the Nnobi,"[383] the ""boy wives" of the Azande and Zulu,"[384] and the woman-woman marriages of the Nuer, and in medieval Japan, Korea and China.[385] And while "not equivalent to same-*gender* couples,"[386] there have also been "marriages between anatomical men, one of whom occupies a trans-gender position,"[387] including among the Native Americans (*berdache*).[388]

Historically, at least since the rise of urbanization and the nation state, men have found ways to have sex with other men, even at risk of their lives; and there is evidence of male meeting places and male sexual liaisons dating at least to the Inquisition.[389] Urbanization and early capitalism facilitated networks of male meeting-places. This phenomenon was only heightened by industrialization and the rise of the individual, instead of the family, wage.

The history of marriage includes same-sex couples, sometimes openly. Before church marriages were performed for a man and a woman, according to the late Yale historian John Boswell, in his landmark book **Same-Sex Unions in Premodern Europe**, ceremonies and liturgy had been first developed for same-sex couples, mostly male, in Europe throughout the medieval period.

In many countries, there are records of individuals hiding their true gender in order to marry someone of the same biological sex. This was the case for Murray Hall, a prominent Tammany politician about the turn of the century. She masqueraded as a man over a 25-year period and married women twice.

During the 1920s, Black lesbian "butch/femme" couples of

Harlem married each other in large wedding ceremonies. The couples obtained marriage licenses by masculinizing a first name or having a gay male surrogate apply for the license.

One of the earliest public forums on same-sex marriage was conducted by The Daughters of Bilitis in 1957. The event, titled "Is a Homophile Marriage Possible?" featured a psychotherapist who answered the question affirmatively.

By the 1960s, "covenant" services for some gay and lesbian couples were conducted by clergy in touch with the *Council on Religion and the Homosexual*. And:

> The first marriage in the nation designed to legally bind two persons of the same sex," claimed an Advocate article published on June 12, 1970. Neva Heckman and Judith Belew were married in Los Angeles by Reverend Troy Perry. Because the couple could not get a state marriage license, the marriage was not, in fact, legally binding.[390]

Few specifics are known about female same-sex relationships in the ancient Western world. Under the feudal model of relationships, women were sometimes able to initiate sexual and emotional intimacy with others in close proximity.[391] As relationships in general were romanticized in the mid-nineteenth century, the romantic friendship model offered women, and men, a fair amount of opportunity for homosocial homoeroticism. The fact that even effusive public displays of affection were not thought sexual between women, meant that women entrapped in familism and the domestic sphere were unlikely to come under suspicion of lesbianism.[392] Prior to the rise of psychology and sexology, women's same-sex sexuality was less policed than men's.

The mid-nineteenth century also saw the rise of sexual freedom movements, including that of the anarchists who espoused "free love," urban middle-class singles, radical youth, feminists, and gay liberationists."[393] Margaret Sanger's hygiene campaign for access to birth control information and contraceptive devices for immigrant and native-born women contributed to the ability of heterosexual, female, free-lovers to conduct themselves with sexual autonomy with less fear of pregnancy. And between the world wars, the early 20th Century German movement for gay male rights began to bear fruit in the U.S. By the end of World War II, gays and lesbians saw the rise of the homophile movement, and there were meeting places and bars in every former American military port.

Modern Same-Sex Relationships

Heterosexual relationships operate under a public "philosophy of marriage . . . based on equality, freedom, and the integrity of the individual conscience."[394] Other-sex couples cohabitate, control their reproduction (plan and prohibit conception), hold a belief in their right to marry for love/romance/affection/ and intimacy, and divorce when their ideals of love and marriage are violated.

Despite liberal sexual freedom movements, at the start of the 21st Century, the desire of some to regulate the sexuality of others has not fully abated.[395] Much of that regulatory concern is directed at gays and lesbians. Some of it is motivated by outright heterosexism and homophobia. Also, some of what passes as concern about same-sex sexuality has as much to do with "changes in the status of women" as with the defense of heterosexual privilege or the fear of (or visceral reaction to) same-sex oriented people and same-sex sexual acts.[396]

Though still complicated (by childbearing, childrearing, economic self-segregation, and employer sexism), the increased equality of women and men in the job force has pulled the rug out from under the mandate of the dependence of women, on marriage, for economic survival.[397] Despite twentieth century secularism and the decline of the power of religious marriage rules, from the late 1970s on, "purity advocates" took up the full-time practice of U.S. politics,[398] making the "defeat [of] gay rights," the prohibition of abortion, and the rollback of contraceptive access, the central foci of their backlash.[399] But the "public marriage philosophies" that affirm sex "for making intimacy" and not just for procreation, and that affirm the contractual and dissoluble nature of marriage as based on "love," are social philosophies that "same-sex couples fit under."[400]

As *Marriage Equality* advocates lead the charge for their right to the legal and social inclusion in "marriage," its "technical definition" remains "difficult to formulate,"[401] in that laws for other-sex couple marriages differ "widely" from state to state on a multitude of issues, including (but not limited to) "common-law marriage . . . [the] grounds for divorce, parental rights over children, and the nature and disposition of communal property."[402]

The marriage equality movement has pressed for inclusion in this conglomeration of state-by-state laws – and worked toward the full dismantling of the reactionary 1996 federal Defense of Marriage Act[403] and a U.S. Supreme Court ruling to reestablish the *Full Faith and Credit*

Clause in regard to state marriage laws – and thus, establish the rights (and responsibilities) of same-sex couples to have their marriages recognized wherever (in the United States) they live.

Yet, the "actual parameters" of other-sex "marriage" remain variable.[404] Whatever the religious beliefs of any given theological stream or sect – the historical fact is that far from being static and universal for the past 5,000+ years – no matter *who* the partners contracting it *or how* – free or arranged, monogamous or polygamous, other-sex or same-sex – "marriage" remains a constantly shifting terrain, always adjusting to social, cultural, and economic shifts in era and epoch.

The Marriage Equality Movement

Looking at the national *Marriage Equality* movement, the first signs of an impetus toward marriage for same-sex couples are seen at, or about, the time of Stonewall within the fledgling gay church movement. In 1969, in San Francisco, the Rev. Troy Perry, founded the *Metropolitan Community Church* (which grew into UFMCC, the *Universal Fellowship of Metropolitan Community Churches*)[405] and began to perform what he termed "holy union" ceremonies.[406] It cannot be said that, early on, the *Metropolitan Community Church* was completely attuned to a monogamy ethic. As well as serving as sites for the origination of the marriage claim, in a community just then expanding past the bar culture, *Metropolitan Community Church* congregations served, and continue to serve, as social centers.[407]

However, the *Metropolitan Community Church* movement has served as "a repository of traditionalism" for more religious and conservative gays and lesbians.[408] And as the AIDS crisis broke in California and New York, *Metropolitan Community Church* congregations served not only to comfort the dying and bury the dead, but as sites that promoted monogamy through religious commitment (*holy union*) ceremonies, and political action.[409]

Also, almost immediately – by the late 1960s/early 1970s – Rev. Perry began to press for legal recognition of these "holy unions." From that time, he has led (and encourages his pastors to lead) annual *Valentine's Day* actions at local courthouses and marriage license bureaus. *Metropolitan Community Church* congregants arrive and request marriage licenses. When they are turned down, they promise the county clerks to return next year.

Perry has often officiated over mass wedding (or *holy union*) ceremonies (with hundreds to thousands of couples), including one on the steps of the Philadelphia Art Museum, and a more well-known one on the steps of the IRS building in Washington D.C., during the 1993 LGBTQ *March on Washington*, and again on the steps of the Lincoln Memorial in 2000 as part of the Millennial March on Washington for Equality.[410] He participates in and encourages couples to press lawsuits seeking legal recognition of their unions.[411]

He filed the first lawsuit for recognition of same-sex couples in 1970.[412] Perry has been continually active in the movement for marriage equality, including activism at every important juncture, increasing the legal movement from the acquisition – and then loss by constitutional amendment – of marriage equality in the state of Hawaii in 1993. After their Canadian wedding (as soon as it became available, July 2003), Rev. Perry and his partner sued the state of California (with the help of well-known attorney, Gloria Allred) for recognition of their legal marriage; and that lawsuit was part of the complex of suits that brought about same-sex marriage in California[413] – before Proposition 8 was passed, and again, in bringing Proposition 8 to the U.S. Supreme Court, where it was struck down – reinstating same-sex marriage in California.

In the wake of the AIDS crisis, by the late 1980s/early 1990s, the "union" idea had caught on, and gay and lesbian couples across the nation began to have *commitment ceremonies*, often with no connection to religion (and without the possibility of connection to law), to dedicate their relationships in the presence of family and friends.[414] However, marriage as a social movement claim didn't take off until after the initial shock of the AIDS crisis. It did not become common for same-sex couples to plan public commitment ceremonies until at least the late 1980s.[415]

1990 saw the foundation of the *Hawai`i Equal Rights Marriage Project* and the *Hawai`i Gay Marriage Project* by the *Gay and Lesbian Education and Advocacy Foundation* of Honolulu. There, three same-sex couples, denied licenses to wed in 1990, filed suit in 1991 against the state on grounds of sex, and sexual orientation, discrimination.

In 1993, the Supreme Court of Hawai`i ruled that marriage could not be denied on the grounds of sex or sexual orientation, and that same-sex couples could not be denied equal protection, without a "compelling public interest." They found no such compelling public interest.

In 1994, the Hawai`ian legislature changed the marriage law to explicitly exclude gay marriage. In 1996, after hearing the appeal, the Supreme Court of Hawai`i ordered the state to issue marriage licenses to same-sex couples, but the State Deputy Attorney General filed a motion to stay the injunction until the appeal was heard. In November of 1998, the voters of Hawai`i amended the state constitution to define marriage as between "one man and one woman," invalidating the same-sex licenses already issued and prohibiting future licenses; and in 1999, the Supreme Court of Hawai`i held that the 1993 case (*Baehr v. Anderson*) was then moot.[416]

Hawai`i had a powerful effect on mobilizing those who opposed same-sex marriage. President Clinton, who had experienced backlash for his initial attempts at rights for gay military service personnel,[417] signed the misnamed federal *Defense of Marriage Act* (or DOMA) in 1996. In rapid succession – to forbid state-level recognition of same-sex unions (civil marriages, civil unions, and domestic partnerships) – forty-one states followed suit and passed state level DOMAs ("*defense of marriage*" acts), and (like Hawaii) – twenty-seven states amended their constitutions. Then, in 2004, then-President George W. Bush called for a federal constitutional amendment.[418]

In 2000, the movement won its first victories. Two legislatures (which had not passed state-level DOMAs or preemptively amended their constitutions) passed relationship recognition bills. Vermont passed a *civil union* bill, and California passed a *domestic partnership* bill. In 2003, the Massachusetts Supreme Judicial Court legalized civil marriage, and the first Massachusetts marriages took place in 2004.[419] Also in 2004, New Jersey passed a more limited domestic partnership bill than California's, but expanded it in 2006, then followed (after a NJ Supreme Court ruling) with a *Civil Union Bill* (December 21· 2006). In 2005, Connecticut granted civil unions. Additionally in 2004, Mayor Gavin Newsom of San Francisco, Mayor Jason West of New Paltz, New York, and Mayor James Bruno of Asbury Park, New Jersey, nearly concurrently, began issuing marriage licenses and performing ceremonies in defiance of their state's laws.[420]

With the many conservative and Republican political victories against same-sex unions, over the approximate decade from Hawaii to Massachusetts, a majority of politicians (even those who may have been private supporters of same-sex rights) exhibited a hesitancy about giving definitive support to same-sex marriage. Some came out in favor of lesser forms of legal protection: anti-discrimination measures, hate crimes bills, and domestic partnerships or civil unions. With the divisive way in which the issue could be used, and the ascendancy of conservative ideologies, even Democrats who privately supported the idea appeared more committed to winning elections than to backing gay constituents. Even in New Jersey, where many political leaders had been willing to come forward in support of civil unions and added transgender individuals in the state's antidiscrimination law, it was clearly perceived as more politically expedient to support civil unions or domestic partnerships, than to support same-sex marriage. At the 2008 election of Barack Obama, California (which had won marriage just months before) lost *marriage equality* to voter passage of Proposition 8. However, the political tide has turned.

In 2008, Connecticut, by state Supreme Court ruling, got same-sex marriage. In 2009, Iowa's Supreme Court overturned that state's ban on same-sex marriage, and Vermont, Maine, and New Hampshire got same-sex marriage by court order. Incumbent President Barack Obama, on February 23, 2011, directed the Department of Justice not to defend DOMA in the Supreme Court case *Hollingsworth v. Perry*, and then (shortly before his reelection) on May 9th, 2012, came out in favor of same-sex marriage (not just lesser relationship recognitions like civil unions). In 2011, New York State granted its gay and lesbian citizens the right to marry the partner of their choice. In 2012, Washington State, Maryland (and Maine) got same-sex marriage by popular vote. In 2013, Rhode Island, Delaware, Minnesota, New Jersey, Hawaii, Illinois, and New Mexico got same-sex marriage.[421] At this writing (May 2015), 37 states recognize same-sex marriage, and the U.S. Supreme Court is presently hearing arguments on the issue.[422]

Conclusion

In the U.S., social movements have grown out of the ideology of inclusion. The founding documents that hypothesized "all" as "created equal" – and the Enlightenment and Rights of the Common Man movement out of which those documents sprang – created the ideological space for those who were not male, or not White, or not propertied, or not of the dominant religion (etc.) to step forward and press into inclusion.

If "all" are created equal, then I am too.

And if I am created equal, then I deserve my shot at the hypothesized "inalienable rights to life, liberty, and the pursuit of happiness" – whatever I understand those to be.

Coming together in collectivities gathered around particular identities has allowed those within a given group to unite in their demand for inclusion in access to that American Dream that preceded the car and the house in the suburbs – that preceded materialism and acquisition – the *Dream of Self-Determination* and freedom from discriminatory barriers to that self-determination.

The engine powering social movements has been, first, coming to consciousness as part of a shared (but in some measure, oppressed or disparaged) identity; second, gathering into groups to discuss the limitations and discriminations experienced; third, strategizing direct actions that will bring the demand for change into the public consciousness and formulating one or more legally-addressable issues and fomenting for the changes in those that you predetermine would improve your collective lot; fourth, standing firm in the face of predictable, but nevertheless, potentially painful and costly backlash; and fifth, staying the course for decades and decades (often 3/4ths of a century and more) until the tide of public opinion (cultural change) turns in your favor and the legal change you have labored for is enacted (carrying more cultural change in its political wake).

Abolitionist and women's rights leader, Lucy Stone said, "To make the public sentiment on the side of all that is just and true and noble is the highest use of life."[423]

Multiple thousands – leaders and rank-and-file – have used their lives in just that way – for the sake of turning the cultural tide of public sentiment to the justice of their cause, thus enacting structural (or political) change.

In more recent times, some voices and much scholarship have sought to complicate the narrative of identity politics.

Yet, identity politics are far from dead – in part, because none of the movements discussed in this piece are over.

One could say that the Abolitionist movement is over. It is true that race-based slavery in the U.S. was brought to an end by the Civil War. One could argue that the Civil Rights Movement ended. And it is true that some progress was made in the desegregation/integration of American society (South *AND* North). But the fact is both of those movements were just bends in a long and flowing stream of Black resistance to oppression that began when the oppression began and continues to this day. And the issues (those historical moments of the continuing movement for Black justice addressed) continue to be – and to need to be – addressed today. Institutional racism and individual prejudice both work out as ongoing acts of discrimination against Black people here, and throughout the African Diaspora, and against other people of color – including (in the U.S.) more recent immigrant groups (Latino/as, Asian). Further, this paper did not address the *American Indian Movement* (AIM), but our national issues with race set their roots in the genocide directed against the indigenous inhabits of this land mass and continues to play out against them in the ongoing theft and defilement (pollution) of their land and water resources, economic disempowerment, and domination by our occupying system of government that turns the declaration of their native sovereignty into meaningless chatter – like the broken treaties still never kept.

Some have said that we are post-feminist now. There have been two primary waves of women's rights activism, one running from 1848 to 1920 and a second running roughly from 1963 into the 1980s. Others say we are in a third wave now.

Underlying these discussions is the truth that women have always been full human beings struggling to manifest the totality of their humanity in whatever settings they found themselves. Women have always worked. In ancient and feudal and modern times, women have always contributed to the sustenance of the lives of their families – and even the 1950s housewife did carework that *was work*.

And the project of recovering women's history has taught us that we have always been there. We have been mystics and prophets and composers and culinary artisans and artists and writers. We have cross-dressed and fought in, and led, armies. We have been queens and heads of tribes and heads of state.

And we have fought for equality of treatment in the public sphere – and in the private. And we still do.

In the window of time between 1920 and 1963, between the 19th Amendment and suffrage and Friedan's "problem that has no name," the movement powered on. Like the African American movement which began with the cessation of the Civil War and continued through the decades of "lifting while climbing" and "freedman's" education into the formation of the NAACP and scores of clubs and associations – until it broke out in the media-watched Civil Rights window – like the African American movement which moved from integration to self-empowerment and Black nationalism and continues on today – women's movement has never stopped.

That which started in Seneca Falls that July afternoon in 1848, didn't stop after women won the vote, but continued on through the 1930s and 40s and 50s: as organizations encouraging women to exercise that right to vote and to press into electoral political positions, as the movement to provide birth control information and develop more reliable methods, as the movement of women into education and careers. And whether we will retrospectively count it as a "wave" or not – whether or not we gain the publicity of media attention – both nationally and globally, women continue to press forward. And continue to need to, as the new form of slavery in the world is the mass trafficking of girls as enslaved (in every sense of the word) subjects in a global sex market.[424]

For those fortunate enough to be on the dominant side of a multiplicity of statuses (native-born and middle class and able-bodied, cisgender, other-sex oriented, etc.), our lived experience has improved. Potentially, we have a good measure of self-determination: opportunities for school and career, the freedom to marry, the freedom to not marry, the freedom to divorce, and the ability to control our reproduction. But all is not well, even for the most fortunate among us. It is not all better now. The strictures of gender roles, the pressures of masculinity and femininity, continue to trouble our other-sex relationships – so that our statistics on the sexual assault of women (and children), and our statistics on intimate partner violence (and the physical assault of children), show that many women's (and children's) lives are a living hell of subordination – even here, in the United States – ever here, for women less likely to be harmed in other ways (trafficked or killed for the family honor or genitally-mutilated) than other women around the globe. No, it is not all better yet. And the movement for women's equality goes on.

The labor movement in the United States achieved great things, helping the working class move into middle class status by the mid-20th Century, ending (in the United States) child labor and sweatshop conditions, and securing a living wage and health care and retirement benefits for millions of American workers. But there is more to be done, as the powers that be were enabled to move those manufacturing jobs offshore, and to reestablish sweatshops, and child labor, and near slave wages in 3rd world arenas.

The U.S. involvement in the war in Vietnam, and involuntary conscription (the draft) in the U.S. military, were brought to an end, but even with a volunteer military, we have never been at peace a moment since World War II.

And this book does not address other compelling movements, like the environmental or anti-nuclear or anti-weapons movements, and many others.

At this writing, the public acceptance of lesbian, gay, bisexual, and transgender people is rising. Both the political, and the cultural coming out movements, are having an effect. Yet, there is still little worse than being perceived to be "gay" in grade school/middle school/and high school, and LGBTQ youth are bullied (face-to-face and cyber-bullied) in overwhelming numbers, and still, frequently, take their own lives because they can't see any way to live as "queer."[425]

Within ongoing movements, social movement organizations (SMOs) continue to work, both on their own group issues and cross-coalitionally, because their goals are not all attained.

The history of U.S. based social movements can never be fully written. Each section and location is full of nuance and terror and valor. This brief overview has not begun to scratch the surface, and I offer my apologies to any group or just cause I have omitted. Let me simply say that, where time alone will not – cannot – bring change, collective active has, and can, and will. Or in the words of Margaret Mead,[426]

Never doubt that a small group of
thoughtful, committed, citizens
can change the world.
Indeed,
it is the only thing that ever has.

Bibliography

A&E/History.com. 2015. *Freedom Summer.* From Foner, Eric and John A. Garraty (eds.). 1991.*The Reader's Companion to American History.* Houghton Mifflin Harcourt Publishing Company. http://www.history.com/topics/black-history/freedom-summer

Adam, Barry D. 1995. *The Rise of a Gay and Lesbian Social Movement.* New York: Twayne Publishers, Simon & Schuster.

AFL-CIO. (accessed) 3May 2015. *Triangle Shirtwaist Fire.* http://www.aflcio.org/Issues/Civil-and-Workplace-Rights/Working-Women/Working-Women-in-Union-History/Triangle-Shirtwaist-Fire

Alba, Richard. D. 1990. *Ethnic Identity: The Transformation of White America.* New Haven: Yale University Press.

Amadiume, Ifi. 1987. *Male Daughters, Female Husbands: Gender and Sex in an African Society.* Atlantic Highlands, NJ: Humanities Press International.

Anderson, Elijah. 1999. *Code of the Street: Decency, Violence, and the Moral Life of the Inner City.* New York: W.W. Norton.

Anderson, John. 2007-2015. *Christiana Riot of 1851.* http://www.blackpast.org/aah/christiana-riot-1851

Anderson, Terry H. 1994. *The Movement and Business* in David Farber. (ed.). "The Sixties: From Memory to History." Chapel Hill: University of North Carolina Press.

Anthony, Susan B, Cady Stanton, Elizabeth, Gge, Matilda Joslyn. (eds.). 1887. *History of Woman Suffrage*, Volume I. http://www.amazon.com/History-Woman-Suffrage-Brownell-Anthony-ebook/dp/B004UJL5SS/ref=sr_1_1?s=digital-text&ie=UTF8&qid=1430704518&sr=1-1

Balwin, James. 21 Dec 1963. *Quote from: A Talk to Teachers*, Saturday Review. In Tim Wise. (2005). *White Like Me.* New York: Soft Skull Press.

Barringer, Mark. 1998. *The Anti-War Movement in the United States.* in Spencer C. Tucker. (ed.). *Encyclopedia of the Vietnam War: A Political, Social, and Military History.* Oxford, UK: ABC-CLIO. http://www.english.uiuc.edu/maps/vietnam/antiwar.html.

Bateman, Geoffrey. 2004 [a]. *Gay Liberation Front.* Chicago: GLBTQ Inc. (Encyclopedia of Gay Lesbian Bisexual Transgender & Queer Culture). http://www.glbtq.com/social-sciences/gay_liberation_front.html

Bateman, Geoffrey. 2004 [b]. *AIDS Activism.* Chicago: GLBTQ Inc. (Encyclopedia of Gay Lesbian Bisexual Transgender & Queer Culture). http://www.glbtq.com/social-sciences/aids_activism.html

Beal, Frances. 1970. *To Be Black and Female.* http://library.duke.edu/rubenstein/scriptorium/wlm/blkmanif/;

Bell, T. Anthony. 20 Feb 2014. *The Quietly Defiant, Unlikely Fighter: Pfc. Sarah Keys and the Fight For Justice And Humanity.* http://www.army.mil/article/120456/The_quietly_defiant__unlikely_fighter ___Pfc__Sarah_Keys_and_the_fight_for_justice_and_humanity/

Bell, Ed. & Lennon, Thomas. 2003. *Unchained Memories: Readings from the Slave Narratives.* [Film] HBO: Home Box Office.

Berger, Joseph. 20 Feb 2011. *100 Years Later, the Roll of the Dead in a Factory Fire Complete.* http://www.nytimes.com/2011/02/21/nyregion/21triangle.html?pagewanted=all&_r=0; http://www.aflcio.org/aboutus/history/history/uprising_fire.cfm

Bérubé. Allan. 1990. *Coming Out Under Fire: The History of Gay Men and Women in World War Two.* New York, The Penguin Group.

BeyondMarriage.Org. 26 July 2006. *Beyond Same-Sex Marriage: A New Strategic Vision For All Our Families & Relationships.* http://www.beyondmarriage.org/full_statement.html.

BIHE (Black Issues in Higher Education). 2005. *The Unfinished Agenda of the Selma-Montgomery Voting Rights March.* (Landmarks in Civil Rights History). Wiley.

Blackwood, Evelyn. 1984. *Sexuality and Gender in Certain Native American Tribes: The Case of Cross-Gender Females.* Signs: Journal of Women in Culture and Society 10(1): 27-42.

Blackwood, Evelyn & Saskia E. Wieringa (eds.). 1999. *Introduction. Female Desires: Same-Sex Relations and Transgender Practices Across Cultures.* New York: Columbia University Press.

Bloom, Amy. 1995/2014. *The Pill Hearings (1970).* The Network News (Jan/Feb 1995 issue). Washington D.C.: National Women's Health Network. http://nwhn.org/pill-hearings-1970-0

Blum, Louise. 2001. *You're Not From Around Here, Are You? A Lesbian in Small Town America.* Madison: University of Wisconsin Press.

Blumberg, Rhoda Lois. 2003. *The Civil Rights Movement.* In Jeff Goodwin & James M. Jasper. (eds.). *The Social Movements Reader: Cases and Concepts.* Malden, MA: Blackwell.

Boston Women's Health Collective. 1970. *Our Bodies, Ourselves.* Boston: Boston Women's Health Book Collective.

Boswell, John. 1994. *Same-Sex Unions in Premodern Europe.* New York: Random House.

Breines, Wini. 1989. *Community and Organization in the New Left, 1962-1968: The Great Refusal.* New Brunswick: Rutgers University Press.

BrightMoments.com. (accessed) 20Apr 2015. *Sojourner Truth.* http://www.brightmoments.com/blackhistory/nsotrue.html

Brinkley, Douglas. 2000. *Mine Eyes Have Seen the Glory: The Life of Rosa Parks.* London: Weidenfeld & Nicolson.

Brinkley, Douglas. 2005. *Rosa Parks: A Life.* NY: Penguin Books.

Bronski, Michael. 2003 [a]. *Pulp Friction: Uncovering the Golden Age of Gay Male Pulps.* New York: St. Martin's Griffin.

Brownmiller, Susan 1975. *Against Our Will: Men, Women and Rape.* New York: Simon & Schuster

Buhle, Mary Jo & Paul Buhle. 1978. *The Concise History of Woman Suffrage (1881-1922): Selections from the Class Work of Stanton, Anthony, Gage, and Harper.* Chicago: University of Illinois Press.

Canetti, Elias. 1966. *Crowds and Power.* New York: Viking Press.

CensusScope.org. (accessed) 29Apr 2015. *Segregation: Dissimilarity Indices. US Metro Areas Ranked by White/Black Dissimilarity Index.* http://www.censusscope.org/us/rank_dissimilarity_white_black.html

Chase, Harry. 2006. *Mixed Train to Providence, A History of the Boston and Providence Rail Road* [etc.]: unpub., Harry B. Chase Jr. papers, Archives and Special Collections, Thomas J. Dodd Center. Storrs, CT: Univ. of Connecticut. (p.294 – original source unknown).

Chase, Harry. 2012. *"Jim Crow" on Massachusetts Passenger Trains.* http://doddcenter.uconn.edu/asc/findaids/Chase/uconn_asc_2003-0037_018.pdf

Chambre, Susan M. 2006. *Fighting for Our Lives: New York's AIDS Community and the Politics of Disease.* (Critical Issues in Health and Medicine). New Brunswick: Rutgers University Press.

Chauncey, George. 2004. *Why Marriage? The History Shaping Today's Debate Over Gay Equality.* New York: Basic Books.

Chibbaro, Jr., Lou. 17 Apr 2013. *Sodomy Laws Remain on Books in 17 States, Including Md. and Va.* The Washington Blade. http://www.washingtonblade.com/2013/04/17/sodomy-laws-remain-on-books-in-17-states-including-md-and-va/

Cohen, Robert, & Reginald E. Zelnik. 2002. *The Free Speech Movement: Reflections on Berkeley in the 1960s.* Berkeley: University of California Press.

Cleaver, Eldridge. 1967.1999. *Soul on Ice.* New York: Delta.

Combahee River Collective. 1977/1979. *A Black Feminist Statement.* In Zillah R. Eisenstein. (ed.). *Capitalist Patriarchy and The Case For Socialist Feminism.* New York: Monthly Review Press.

Coontz, Stephanie. 1998. *The Way We Really Are: Coming to Terms With America's Changing Families.* New York: Basic Books.

Coontz, Stephanie. 2000. *The Way We Never Were: American Families and the Nostalgia Trap.*

Coontz, Stephanie. 2005. *Marriage, a History: From Obedience to Intimacy or How Love Conquered Marriage.* New York: Viking/Penguin.

Corey, Daniel Webster. 1951. *The Homosexual in America: A Subjective Approach.* New York: Greenberg.

Cott, Nancy. 2000. *Public Vows: A History of Marriage and The Nation.* Cambridge: Harvard University Press.

DarbyHistory.com. (accessed) 29Apr 2015. *William Still, Darby, and the Desegregation of Philadelphia Streetcars.* http://www.darbyhistory.com/Still-StreetcarStruggle.html

Demian. 10 Jul 2011. *Legal Marriage Court Cases — A Timeline: U.S. Court Cases from 1971 to the Present.* http://buddybuddy.com/t-line-1.html

Demian. 2015. *Legal Marriage Notes: An International Resource for Same-sex Couples.* Seattle: Partners Task Force for Gay & Lesbian Couples. http://buddybuddy.com/partners.html

D'Emilio, John. 2003. *The Gay Liberation Movement.* In J. Goodwin & J. M. Jasper. *The Social Movements Reader: Cases and Concepts.* (pp32-37). Malden, MA: Blackwell.

D'Emilio, John & Estelle Freedman. 1988. *Intimate Matters: A History of Sexuality in America.* New York: Perennial/ Harper & Row.

Douglass, Frederick. 1855. *My Bondage and My Freedom.* NY: Miller, Orton & Mulligan. (repub. 1987. Urbana & Chicago, IL: University of Illinois Press.)

Douglass, Frederick. In Chase, Harry. 2012. *"Jim Crow" on Massachusetts Passenger Trains.* http://doddcenter.uconn.edu/asc/findaids/Chase/uconn_asc_2003-0037_018.pdf

DuBois, Ellen Carol. 1998. Woman Suffrage & Women's Rights. New York: NYU Press. [Kindle Edition] http://www.amazon.com/Woman-Suffrage-Womens-Rights-DuBois-ebook/dp/B00EIFPDW8/ref=sr_1_8?ie=UTF8&qid=1392753527&sr=8-8&keywords=ellen+carol+dubois

Dupre, Jeffrey. 1998. *Out of the Past: The Struggle for Gay and Lesbian Rights in America*. [Film]. Allumination Studio.

Ehrenreich, Barbara. 2001. *Nickel and Dimed*. New York: Metropolitan, Owl, Henry Holt.

EJI (Equal Justice Initiative) 2014. *Lynching In America: Confronting The Legacy Of Racial Terror*. Montgomery, AL. http://www.eji.org/lynchinginamerica

Ennen, Edith. 1989. *The Medieval Woman*. (translation by Edmund Jephcott). Cambridge, MA: Basil Blackwell.

Equality Matters (Staff). 19 Apr 2011. *"Homosexual Conduct" Still Illegal In Fourteen States*. http://equalitymatters.org/blog/201104190002

Evans, Lauren. 15 Sep 2006. *A Brief History of Women's Health Specialists*. Women's Health Specialists (a.k.a. The Feminist Women's Health Centers of California). http://www.womenshealthspecialists.org/about-us/history

Evans, Sara. 1989/1997. *Born for Liberty*. New York: Free Press, Simon & Schuster.

Evans-Pritchard, E.E. 1970. *Sexual Inversion Among the Azande*. American Anthropologist 72: 1428-34.

Explore PAHistory.com [1st Protest]. 2011/(accessed) 3May 2015. *First Protest Against Slavery Historical Marker*. WITF.

Explore PAHistory.com [Whittier]. (accessed) 3May 2015. *John Greenleaf Whittier, circa 1860*. http://explorepahistory.com/displayimage.php?imgId=1-2-F80

ExplorePAhistory.com [Christiana Riot]. 2011/(accessed) 3May 2015. *The Christiana Riot Historical Marker*. WITF. http://explorepahistory.com/hmarker.php?markerId=1-A-109

Faderman, Lillian. 1981. *Surpassing the Love of Men*. New York: Quality Paperback Book.

Faderman, Lillian. 1999/2000. *To Believe in Women: What Lesbians Have Done for America—A History*. New York: Houghton Mifflin/First Mariner Books.

Fanon, Frantz. 1991. *Black Skin, White Masks*. (translation by Constance Farrington). New York: Grove Press.

Farber, David. (ed.). 1994. *The Sixties: From Memory to History*. (Introduction). Chapel Hill: University of North Carolina Press.

Feagin, Joe R. 2001. *Racist America: Roots, Current Realities, and Future Reparations*. New York: Routledge.

Forrest, Katherine V. 2005. *Lesbian Pulp Fiction: The Sexually Intrepid World of Lesbian Paperback Novels 1950-1965*. Cleis Press.

Frankenberg, Ruth. 1993. *White Women, Race Matters: The Social Construction of Whiteness*. Minneapolis: University of Minnesota Press.

Free Library of Philadelphia. 2015. *Barbara Gittings Collection*. http://libwww.freelibrary.org/explore/shell.cfm?topicTitle=GLBT&template =gittings.cfm

FreedomtoMarry.org. 2003-2015. *The Defense of Marriage Act*. http://www.freedomtomarry.org/states/entry/c/doma

Freeman, Jo. 1971/(accessed) 4May 2015. *The Women's Liberation Movement: Its Origins, Structures and Ideals*. Duke University Libraries Digital Collection. http://library.duke.edu/digitalcollections/wlmpc_wlmms01013/

Freeman, Jo. 2004 [a]. *The Berkeley Free Speech Movement*. in Immanual Ness (ed.). "Encyclopedia of American Social Movements." (pp1178-1182). Armonk, NY: M.E. Sharpe. http://www.jofreeman.com/sixtiesprotest/berkeley.htm

Freeman, Jo. 2004 [b]. *At Berkeley in the Sixties: The Education of an Activist, 1961-1965*. Bloomington: University of Indiana Press.

Gamson, Joshua. 2003. *The Dilemmas of Identity Politics*. in Jeff Goodwin & James M. Jasper (eds.). *The Social Movements Reader: Cases and Concepts*. Malden, MA: Blackwell. 2003:335-44.

Gates, Henry Louis; Crew, Spencer; & Cynthia Goodman. 2003. *Unchained Memories: Readings from the Slave Narratives*. Bullfinch.

Gazit, Chana (dir.). 2003. *American Experience. The Pill: Sex, Religion, Politics. It Changed Everything*. [Film]. Steward/Gazit Productions, Inc. for American

Experience, Public Broadcasting Service.
http://www.pbs.org/wgbh/amex/pill/filmmore/fd.html#

Gibson, Robert A. 2015. *The Negro Holocaust: Lynching and Race Riots in the United States,1880-1950*. YNHTI (Yale-New Haven Teachers Institute).
http://www.yale.edu/ynhti/curriculum/units/1979/2/79.02.04.x.html

Gies, Frances and Gies, Joseph. 1987. *Marriage and Family in the Middle Ages. (1st ed.)*. New York: Harper and Row.

Goodman, Barak & John Maggio. (dirs). 2004. *Kinsey: American Experience*. [Film]. PBS. Ark Media, Twin Cities Public Television.

Goodreads. 2015. *Margaret Mead > Quotes*.
www.goodreads.com/author/quotes/61107.Margaret_Mead

Goodwin, Jeff & James M. Jasper (eds.). 2003. *The Social Movements Reader: Cases and Concepts*. Malden, MA: Blackwell.

Goldstein, Steven. 25 Oct 2006. *Fieldnotes*. Garden State Equality "Day of Decision" Rally, Montclair, N.J

Gonzalez, Alejandro. 2 Dec 2013. *Same Sex Weddings Begin in Hawaii: Most States Still Ban Gay Marriage*. The Associated Press.: USA Today.
http://www.usatoday.com/story/news/nation/2013/12/02/gay-weddings-hawaii/3801123/

Gordis, D.H. 1993. *Marriage: Judaism's "Other" Covenant Relationship."* In Rela M. Geffen. (ed.). *Celebration and Renewal: Rites of Passage in Judaism*. (pp90-123). Philadelphia: The Jewish Publication Society.

Goulet, Jean_Guy. 1996. *The 'Berdache'/ 'Two-Spirit:' A Comparison of Anthropological and Native Constructions of Gender*. Journal of the Royal Anthropological Institute. 2(4):683-702.

Graff, E.J. 1999. *What Is Marriage For?* Boston: Beacon Press.

Graff, E. J. 2005. *Interview*. In Jim de Sève, Constance Rodgers, & Stephen Pelletier. (eds.). *Tying the Knot*. [Film] 1049 Films: New View Video.

Haber, Louis. 1970. *Black Pioneers of Science and Invention*. New York: Odyssey/Harcourt Brace & Company.

Hagenmayer, S. Joseph. 3 Dec 1998. *Carolyn Moore, 82, A Civil-Rights Leader.* Philadelphia Inquirer. http://articles.philly.com/1998-12-03/news/25722973_1_philadelphia-transit-naacp-civil-rights

Halsall, Paul. 1996. *The Canons of the Fourth Lateran Council, 1215.* Medieval Sourcebook: Twelfth Ecumenical Council: Lateran IV 1215. http://www.fordham.edu/halsall/basis/lateran4.asp

Hamilton, Charles & Carmichael, Stokely (Kwame Ture). 1967/1992. *Black Power: The Politics of Liberation.* New York: Vintage.

Hampton, Henry. 1986. *Eyes on the Prize Series.* Blackside Inc.

Hampton, Henry & Steve Fayer. 1990. *Voices of Freedom: An Oral History of the Civil Rights Movement from the 1950s through the 1980s.* (Blackside: Voices of Freedom). NY: Bantam/Doubleday/Dell. (p.17-18 & 22).

Harrell, Antoinette. 2014. *Department of Justice: Slavery, Involuntary Servitude, and Peonage.* Antoinette Harrell.

Hartog, Hendrik. 2000. *Man & Wife in America: A History.* Cambridge: Harvard University Press.

Halsall, Paul. 1997/(accessed) 2 May 2015. *Modern History Sourcebook: Harriet Robinson: Lowell Mill Girls.* http://www.fordham.edu/halsall/mod/robinson-lowell.html

Hendrix, Lewellyn. 1997. *Quality and Equality in Marriage: A Cross-Cultural View.* Cross-Cultural Research 31(3):201-225.

Hill Collins, Patricia. 2000. *Black Feminist Thought: Knowledge, Consciousness, and the Politics of Empowerment.* New York: Routledge.

Hilty, James. 13 Sep 2006. *Higher Education and the Constitution: A Match or Mismatch?* Ambler, PA: Public Address, Bright Hall Lounge.

Hinsch, Brent. 1990. *Passion of the Cut Sleeve: The Male Homosexual Tradition in China.* Berkeley and Los Angeles: University of California Press.

History.com. 2015. *The Christiana Riot: 1851.* http://www.history.com/this-day-in-history/the-christiana-riot

HistoryMakingProductions.com. 26 Apr 2011 [airdate]. *Philadelphia: The Great Experiment, Episode 1 (The Floodgates Open (1865-1876)*. (Transcript: Minute 13:40 →17:25) http://historymakingproductions.com

HistoryMakingProductions.com. 24 Jan 2013 [airdate]. *Philadelphia: The Great Experiment, Episode 3 (Promise for a Better City (1944-1964)*. (Transcript: Minute 1:33 → 4:17). http://historymakingproductions.com

HistoryWiz.com. (accessed) 2 May 2015. *The Boston Slave Riot*. http://www.historywiz.com/bostonriot.htm

Hoffer, Eric. 1951/1966. *The True Believer*. New York: Harper & Row.

hooks, bell. (984/2000. *Feminist Theory (2nd ed.)*. Cambridge, MA: South End Press.

Hoose, Phillip. 2010. *Claudette Colvin: Twice Toward Justice*. Square Fish; Reprint edition.

HRC.org. 4 May 2015. *The HRC Story: About Us*. http://www.hrc.org/the-hrc-story/about-us

iampunha. 17 Jan 2014. *Separate: 117 Years of Fighting Transportation Segregation*. http://www.dailykos.com/story/2014/01/18/1270537/-Separate-117-years-of-fighting-transportation-segregation#

IGIC (International Gay Information Center). (accessed) 4 May 2015. *Gay Activist Alliance: Historical Note*. http://microformguides.gale.com/Data/Introductions/20240FM.htm

Inness, Sherrie A. 2002. *Novel: Lesbian*. Chicago: GLBTQ Inc. (Encyclopedia of Gay Lesbian Bisexual Transgender & Queer Culture). http://www.glbtq.com/literature/novel_lesbian.html

Jamieson, Kathleen Hall. 1995. *Beyond the Double Bind: Women and Leadership*. New York: Oxford University Press.

Jasper, James M. & Dorothy Nelkin. 1992. *The Animal Rights Crusade: The Growth of a Moral Protest*. New York: Free Press.

jessamyn. 30 Mar 2013. *Barbara Gittings, that Lady in the "Hug a Homosexual" Booth*. Librarian.net. http://www.librarian.net/stax/4070/barbara-gittings-that-lady-in-the-hug-a-homosexual-booth/

109

Johnson, Ramon. *2015. How Many Soldiers Have Been Discharged Since Don't Ask, Don't Tell Was Enacted?* http://gaylife.about.com/od/dontaskdonttell/f/discharged.htm

Kaczorowski, Craig. 2002. *Aids Activism in the Arts.* Chicago: GLBTQ Inc. (Encyclopedia of Gay Lesbian Bisexual Transgender & Queer Culture). http://www.glbtq.com/arts/aids_activism_art.html

Katz, Jonathan. 1976. *Gay American History: Lesbians and Gay Men in the U.S.A.* New York: Thomas Y. Crowell.

Kelley, Blair L. 2010. *Right to Ride: Streetcar Boycotts and African American Citizenship in the Era of Plessy v. Ferguson.* (John Hope Franklin Series in African American History and Culture). Chapel Hill, NC: University of North Carolina Press.

Kepner, Jim & Stephen O. Murray. 2002. *Henry Gerber (1895-1972): Grandfather of the American Gay Movement.* In Vern L. Bullough (ed). *Before Stonewall: Activists for Gay and Lesbian Rights in Historical Context.* New York: Routledge.

Kitchell, Mark. (prod./dir.). & Veronica Selver. (ed.). 1990. *"Berkeley in the Sixties."* Kitchell Films with P.O.V. Theatrical Films. 1990.

Knight, Kevin. 2010. *The Sacrament of Marriage.* New Advent Catholic Encyclopedia. http://www.newadvent.org/cathen/09707a.htm

Kornhauser, William. 1959. *The Politics of Mass Society.* Glencoe, IL: The Free Press.

Kotulski, Davina. 2004. *Why You Should Give a Damn About Gay Marriage.* Los Angeles: Advocate Books/Alyson Press.

Lambda Legal. 4 May 2015. *About Us.* http://www.lambdalegal.org/about-us

Lapham, Thea Rozetta. (accessed) 3 May 2015 [a]. *Sojourner TruthA Life Led By Faith.* SojournerTruth.org. http://www.sojournertruth.org/library/archive/LifeLedByFaith.htm

Lapham, Thea Rozetta. (accessed) 3 May 2015 [b]. *Sojourner Truth and Rosa Parks:Sisters in a 90-Year Struggle.* SojournerTruth.org. http://www.sojournertruth.org/library/archive/SojournerAndParks.htm

Lawrence, Michael Anthony. 2010. *Radicals in their Own Time: Four Hundred Years of Struggle for Liberty and Equal Justice in America*. Cambridge University Press. (p139).

Leacock, Eleanor. 1978. *Women's Status in Egalitarian Society: Implications for Social Evolution*. Current Anthropology 19(2): 247-275.

Levi-Strauss, C. 1969. *The Raw and the Cooked: Introduction to a Science of Mythology*. (translation by I. J. & D. Weightman). New York: Harper Torchbooks.

Libcom.org. (accessed) 28 Jan 2014. *The Ludlow Massacre: 1914*. http://libcom.org/history/1914-the-ludlow-massacre

Lipsitz, George. 1998. *The Possessive Investment in Whiteness: How White People Profit from Identity Politics*. Philadelphia: Temple University Press.

Lorde, Audre. 1983. *There is No Hierarchy of Oppression*. In "Homophobia and Education." New York: Council on Interracial Books for Children. Bulletin 14. Retrieved from: http://uuliveoak.org/pdfs/worship_9-04-09_excerpts_no_hierarchy_of_oppressions.pdf

Lorde, Audre. 1984. *Scratching the Surface: Some Notes on Barriers to Woman and Loving*. In Audre Lorde. *Sister Outsider: Essays and Speeches* (pp45-52). Freedom, CA: Crossing Press Feminist Series.

Mabee, Carleton. 1995. *Sojourner Truth , Slave, Prophet, Legend*. NY: New York University Press.

Marcus Garvey Tribute. 2014. *The Life and Legacy of Marcus Garvey*. http://www.marcusgarvey.com

Margolin, Emma. 14 Feb 2014. *Republicans Introduce a Bill That Looks a Lot Like DOMA*. NBC Universal. http://www.msnbc.com/msnbc/ted-cruz-anti-gay-legislation

McAdam, Doug. 1982. *Political Process and the Development of Black Insurgency, 1930-1970*. Chicago: University of Chicago Press

McAdam, Doug, John D. McCarthy, & Mayer N. Zald. (eds.). 1996. *Comparative Perspectives on Social Movements: Political Opportunities, Mobilizing Structures, and Cultural Framings*. New York: Cambridge University Press.

McClintock, Anne. 1995. *No Longer in a Future Heaven: Nationalism, Gender and Race*. In Anne McClintock. (ed.). *Imperial Leather: Race, Gender, and Sexuality in the Colonial Context*. (pp352-389). New York: Routledge.

McGarry, Molly & Fred Wasserman. 1998. *Becoming Visible: An Illustrated History of Lesbian and Gay Life in Twentieth-Century America*. New York: Penguin Putnam.

McIntosh, Peggy. 1989. *White Privilege: Unpacking the Invisible Knapsack*. In Peggy McIntosh. *Working Paper 189: White Privilege and Male Privilege: A Personal Account of Coming to See Correspondences through Work in Women's Studies*.

McKay, Rich. 10 Feb 2015. *The History Of Lynching In America Is Worse Than You Think, Says Study*. Reuters/Huffington Post. http://www.huffingtonpost.com/2015/02/10/history-of-lynching-us-worse_n_6656604.html

MCC (Metropolitan Community Church). 2013 [a]. *History of MCC*. http://mccchurch.org/overview/history-of-mcc/

MCC (Metropolitan Community Church). 2013 [b]. *MCC and Marriage Equality: Timeline*. http://mccchurch.org/overview/history-of-mcc/mcc-and-marriage-equality/

MCC (MCC (Metropolitan Community Church). 4 May 2015. *Weddings and Holy Unions: Founders MCC*. http://www.mccla.org/life-ceremonies/weddings-holy-unions/

Melucci, Alberto. 1996. *Challenging Codes*. New York: Cambridge University Press.

Michels, Tony. 1996-2014. *Uprising of 20,000 (1909)*. Jewish Women's Archive: Jewish Women, A Comprehensive Historical Encyclopedia. http://jwa.org/encyclopedia/article/uprising-of-20000-1909

Moraga, Cherrie & Gloria Anzaldua. 1984. *This Bridge Called My Back: Writings by Radical Women of Color*. (2nd ed.). Kitchen Table, Women of Color Press.

Murray, Stephen O. 2000. *Homosexualities*. Chicago: The University of Chicago Press.

NAACP. 2009-2015 [a]. *NAACP: 100 Years Of History*
http://www.naacp.org/pages/naacp-history

NAACP. 2009-2015 [b]. *NAACP Legal History.*
http://www.naacp.org/pages/naacp-legal-history

National Archives. (accessed) 29 Apr 2015. *Separate is Not Equal: Brown v. Board of Education.* Washington, D.C.: Smithsonian National Museum of American History. http://americanhistory.si.edu/brown/history/1-segregated/separate-but-equal.html

National Archives. (accessed) 3 May 2015. *African American Heritage: The Freedmen's Bureau, 1865-1872.*
http://www.archives.gov/research/african-americans/freedmens-bureau/

National LGBTQ Task Force. 4 May 2015. *About: Mission & History.*
http://www.thetaskforce.org/about/mission-history.html

NWHP (National Women's History Project). (accessed) 4 May 2015. *Writing Women Back Into History.* http://www.nwhp.org/aboutnwhp/

OHM. 2013. *An Unsung Hero in the Fight for Civil Rights: A Story of Quiet Courage.* Our Heritage Magazine. http://ourheritagemagazine.com/our-heritage-magazine-online/sarah-louise-keys/

Painter, Nell Irvin. 1996. *Sojourner Truth: A Life, A Symbol.* New York: W.W. Norton.

PBS. (accessed) 11 Feb 2014. *Out of the Past: Henry Gerber.*
http://www.pbs.org/outofthepast/past/p3/gerber.html

PBS. 2015. *Historical Documents: Executive Committee of Pennsylvania Anti-Slavery Society.* Africans in America: Judgment Day.
http://www.pbs.org/wgbh/aia/part4/4h1544.html

Peck, Ira. 2015. *Lucretia Mott: Woman of Courage.* Scholastic, Inc.
http://www.scholastic.com/browse/article.jsp?id=4953

Perry, Troy. 26 Jan 2006 [a]. *A Message From The Reverend Dr. Troy D. Perry For Same-Sex Marriage Rights.*
MCCChurch.org.http://www.mcchurch.org/AM/Template.cfm?Section=Search&template=/CM/HTMLDisplay.cfm&ContentID=1333

Perry, Troy. 25 Mar 2006 [b]. *Public Address on the 5th Anniversary of the Imago Dei Metropolitan Community Church.* Glen Mills, PA: Gradyville United Methodist Church Facility.

Perry-Wood, Lisa (Ex. Dir.). 2010. *The Commonwealth of Massachusetts Commission on Gay, Lesbian, Bisexual and Transgender Youth: Annual Report.* Boston: Administrative Office c/o MA DPH - 250 Washington Street - 4th floor. www.mass.gov/cgly

Pharr, Suzanne. 1977. Homophobia: A Weapon of Sexism. Berkeley: Chardon Press.

Phibbs, Cheryl. 2009. *The Montgomery Bus Boycott: A History and Reference Guide.* Greenwood.

Polaris Project. 2015 [a]. Sex Trafficking in the U.S. http://www.polarisproject.org/human-trafficking/sex-trafficking-in-the-us

Polaris Project. 2015 [b]. Labor Trafficking in the U.S. http://www.polarisproject.org/human-trafficking/labor-trafficking-in-the-us

Pratt, Gary D. 2004-2006. *Social Sciences: Philadelphia.* Chicago: GLBTQ Inc. (Encyclopedia of Gay Lesbian Bisexual Transgender & Queer Culture). http://www.glbtq.com/social-sciences/philadelphia.html

Railroad Museum of Pennsylvania. (accessed) 30 Apr 2015. *Tears, Trains and Triumphs: The Historical Legacy of African-Americans and Pennsylvania's Railroads.* http://www.rrmuseumpa.org/about/rrpeopleandsociety/legacy.shtml

Ring, Trudy. 17 Apr 2013. *Texas May Finally Repeal Sodomy Law: The Repeal Would Come 10 Years After the Law was Declared Unconstitutional. Several Other States Still Have Sodomy Laws on the Books as Well.* http://www.advocate.com/politics/2013/04/17/texas-may-finally-repeal-sodomy-law

Robertson, Campbell 10 Feb 2015. *History of Lynchings in the South Documents Nearly 4,000 Names.* NY: NY Times. http://www.nytimes.com/2015/02/10/us/history-of-lynchings-in-the-south-documents-nearly-4000-names.html?_r=0

Robinson, Jo Ann Gibson. 1987. *The Montgomery Bus Boycott and the Women Who Started It: The Memoir of Jo Ann Gibson Robinson*. Knoxville: University of Tennessee Press.

Rosario, Vernon A. 2002. *Homosexuality and Science: A Guide to the Debates*. (p74). Santa Barbara, CA: ABC-CLIO, Inc.

Royce, Edward. 1993. *The Origins of Southern Sharecropping*. (Labor and Social Change). Philadelphia: Temple University Press.

Rubin, G. 1975. *The Traffic in Women: Notes of the 'Political Economy' of Sex*. In R. R. Reiter. (ed.). *Toward an Anthropology of Women*. (pp157-210). New York: Monthly Review Press.

Rubin, Gayle. 1984. *Thinking Sex: Notes for a Radical Theory of the Politics of Sexuality*. In C. S. Vance. (ed.). *Pleasure and Danger: Exploring Female Sexuality*. (pp267-319). London: Pandora Press.

Rupp, Leila J. 1999. *A Desired Past: A Short History of Same-Sex Love in America*. Chicago: University of Chicago Press.

Rupp, Leila J. & Taylor, Verta. 1987. *Survival in the Doldrums: The American Women's Rights Movement, 1945 to the 1960s*. New York: Oxford University Press.

Russo, Vito. 1981/1987. *The Celluloid Closet: Homosexuality in the Movies*. New York: Harper & Row.

Sargeant, Fred. 22 Jun 2010. *A First-Person Account of the First Gay Pride March: 1970 (Remembering the March, A Year After the Stonewall Riots)*. http://www.villagevoice.com/2010-06-22/news/1970-a-first-person-account-of-the-first-gay-pride-march/full/

SCBorromeo.org. (accessed) 4 May 2015. *The Marriage Covenant*. Catechism: St. Charles Borromeo.http://www.scborromeo.org/ccc/para/1660.htm

Scagliotti, John. (dir.). 2003. *Dangerous Living: Coming Out in The Developing World*. [Film] US: After Stonewall, Inc. First Run Features. http://firstrunfeatures.com/dangerousliving.html

Shapiro, J. R. 1984. *Marriage Rules, Marriage Exchange, and the Definition of Marriage in Lowland South America*. In Kenneth M. Kensinger. (ed.). *Marriage*

Practices in Lowland South America. (pp1-30). Urbana and Chicago: University of Illinois Press.

Schiller, Greta & Rosenberg, Robert (dirs). 1984. *Before Stonewall*. [Film]. Before Stonewall, Inc., Center for the Study of Filmed History.

Schnapp, Jeffery & Matthew Tiews. (eds.). 2006. *Crowds*. Palo Alto: Stanford University Press.

Schneider, David M. 1980. *American Kinship: A Cultural Account*. Chicago: University of Chicago Press.

SDSU (San Diego State University). (last update) 20 Jan 2015. *History: Beginnings of a Women's Movement. Women's Studies*. http://www-rohan.sdsu.edu/~wsweb/history.htm

Seale, Bobby. 1970/1997. *Seize the Time: The Story of the Black Panther Party and Huey P. Newton*. Baltimore: Black Classic Press.

Shapiro, J. R. 1984. *Marriage Rules, Marriage Exchange, and the Definition of Marriage in Lowland South America*. In Kenneth M. Kensinger. (ed.). *Marriage Practices in Lowland South America*. (pp1-30). Urbana and Chicago: University of Illinois Press.

Silverblatt, Irene Marsha. 1987. *Moon, Sun, and Witches: Gender Ideologies and Class in Inca and Colonial Peru*. Princeton: Princeton University Press.

Silverman, Victor & Stryker, Susan (dirs). 2005. *Screaming Queens: The Riot at Compton's Cafeteria*. [Film]. Frameline Studio.

Singer, Bennett. & Nancy Kates, Rhonda Collins, David Petersen. 2006. *POV: Brother Outsider: The Life of Bayard Rustin*. The National Black Programming Consortium. Point of View. California Newsreel.

SLATE Archives.org. 2003-2005. *The Beginning of the New Left: The History of SLATE: UC Berkeley 1950s/1960s*. http://www.slatearchives.org/history.htm

Stacey, Judith. 1990/1998. *Brave New Families: Stories of Domestic Upheaval in Late-Twentieth-Century America*. Berkeley: University of California Press.

Stacey, Judith. 2002. *Gay and Lesbian Families Are Here; All Our Families Are Queer: Let's Get Used to It!* (pp395-407). In Christine L. Williams & Arlene Stein. *Sexuality and Gender*. Malden, MA: Blackwell Publishers.

Stannard, Una. 1977. *Mrs. Man.* San Franciso: Germainbooks.

Steakley, James. 1993. *The Homosexual Emancipation Movement in Germany.* Beaufort Books.

Stein, Arlene. 1997. *Sex and Sensibility: Stories of a Lesbian Generation.* Berkeley: University of California Press.

Steinem, Gloria. 2006. In Paola di Florio. *Home of the Brave: Viola Liuzzo.* [Film]. Home Vision Entertainment.

Stolcke, Verne. 1993. *Is Sex to Gender as Race is to Ethnicity?* In T. del Valle. (ed.). *Gendered Anthropology.* (pp17-37). New York: Routledge.

Stoler, A. L. 1989. *Making Empire Respectable: The Politics of Race and Sexual Morality in 20th Century Cultures.* American Ethnologist 16(4): 634-660.

Stone, S. 1999. *Hippies from A to Z: Their Sex, Drugs, Music and Impact On Society From The Sixties To The Present.* Buffalo, New York: High Interest Publishing.

Sullivan-Blum, Constance R. 2003. *"The Two Shall Become One Flesh:" The Same-Sex Marriage Debate in Mainline Christianity.* Dissertation: State University of New York, Binghamton.

Tarrow, Sidney. 1994. *Power in Movement: Social Movements, Collective Action and Politics.* New York: Cambridge University Press.

Tarrow, Sidney. 1998. *Power in Movement: Social Movements and Contentious Politics.* New York: Cambridge University Press.

Tatum, Beverly Daniel. 1997. *Why Are All the Black Kids Sitting Together in the Cafeteria? and Other Conversations About Race.* New York: Basic Books.

Temple University Library. (accessed) 28 Apr 2015. *Timeline: The Life and Times of William Still (1821-1902); William Still: An African-American Abolitionist.* Philadelphia: Temple University Library. http://stillfamily.library.temple.edu/timeline/william-still

Theoharis, Jeanne. 2014.*The Rebellious Life of Mrs. Rosa Parks.*Beacon Press.

Theoharis, Jeanne (author), Komozi Woodard (author), & Dayo Gore (ed.). 2009. *Want to Start a Revolution?: Radical Women in the Black Freedom Struggle.* NY: NYU Press.

Thomas, Wesley & Jacobs, Sue-Ellen. 1999 '. . . *And We Are Still Here:' From Berdache to Two-Spirit People.* American Indian Culture & Research Journal. 23(2):91-108.

Tilly, Charles. 2004. *Social Movements, 1768-2004.* Boulder, CO: Paradigm Publishers.

Timmons, Stuart. 1990. *The Trouble With Harry Hay: Founder of the Modern Gay Movement.* Los Angeles: Alyson.

Touraine, A. 1977/1985. *An Introduction to the Study of Social Movements.* Social Research, 52, 749-87.

Trenholm State Technical College Archives. (accessed) 30Apr 2015. *Biographical Sketch of Aurelia Eliseera Shine Browder (Coleman).* Montgomery Bus Boycott: Dr. Gwen Patton Collection. http://www.crmvet.org/info/mbbbios.htm

Tutu, Archbishop Desmond. 2005. In Tim Wise. *White Like Me: Reflection on Race from a Privileged Son.* New York: Soft Skull Press. P.153

U.E. News. 2003. *The Great Strike of 1877.* United Electrical Workers News. http://www.ranknfile-ue.org/uen_1877.html

UMWA. (accessed) 28 Jan 2014. *UMWA History: The Ludlow Massacre.* United Mine Workers of America: AFL-CIO, CLC. http://www.umwa.org/?q=content/ludlow-massacre;

u-s-history.com. 2015. *Lynching.* http://www.u-s-history.com/pages/h4047.html

Van Grubbs, Judith E. 1994. *'Pagan' and 'Christian' Marriage: The State of the Question.* Journal of Early Christian Studies 2(3):361-412.

van Onselen, C. 1984. *The Small Matter of a Horse: The Life of "Nongoloza" Mathebula, 1867-1948.* Johannesburg: Ravan.

Warner, Michael. 1999. *The Trouble with Normal: Sex, Politics, and the Ethics of Queer Life.* Cambridge, MA: Harvard University Press.

Warner, R. Stephen. 2002. *The Metropolitan Community Churches and the Gay Agenda: The Power of Pentecostalism and Essentialism.* (pp281-295). In Christine L. Williams & Arlene Stein. *Sexuality and Gender.* Malden, MA: Blackwell Publishers

Warshaw, Robin 1988. *I Never Called It Rape: The Ms. Report on Recognizing, Fighting, and Surviving Date and Acquaintance Rape.* New York: Harper.

Waterworth, J. 1848/(accessed) 4 May 2015. *Canons and Decrees of the Sacred and Oecumenical Council of Trent: Twenty-Fourth Session.* London: Dolman. (Scanned 1995 Hanover.Edu). http://history.hanover.edu/texts/trent/ct24.html

WDN (Washington Daily News). 7 Feb 2012. *The Legacy of Sarah Keys.* http://www.thewashingtondailynews.com/2012/02/07/the-legacy-of-sarah-keys-20712/

Weeks, Jeffrey. 1977. *Coming Out: Homosexual Politics in Britain, From the Nineteenth Century to the Present.* Quartet Books.

Weeks, Jeffrey. 1981/1989. *Sex Politics and Society: The Regulation of Sexuality Since 1800.* (revised). Longman.

Wells, T. 1998. *The Anti-War Movement in the United States. In The Oxford Companion to American Military History.* Oxford: Oxford University Press. http://www.english.uiuc.edu/maps/vietname/antiwar.html.

Whelehan, Imelda. 1995. *Modern Feminist Thought: From the Second Wave to "Post Feminism."* Edinburgh University Press.

Whittier, John Greenleaf. 1872/(accessed) 3 May 2015. *The Pennsylvania Pilgrim (poem).* http://www.poemhunter.com/poem/the-pennsylvania-pilgrim/

Wikipedia. (modified) 7 Feb 2015. *Philadelphia Transit Strike of 1944.* http://en.wikipedia.org/wiki/Philadelphia_transit_strike_of_1944

Wikipedia. (modified) 10 Feb 2015. *Keys v. Carolina Coach Co.* http://en.wikipedia.org/wiki/Keys_v._Carolina_Coach_Co.

Wikipedia. (modified) 9 Mar 2015. *SLATE.* http://en.wikipedia.org/wiki/SLATE

Wikipedia. (modified) 15 Mar 2015. *Irene Morgan*.
http://en.wikipedia.org/wiki/Irene_Morgan

Wikipedia. (modified) 16 Mar 2015 [a]. *Aurelia Browder*.
http://en.wikipedia.org/wiki/Aurelia_Browder

Wikipedia. (modified) 16 Mar 2015 [b]. *Mary Louise Smith*.
http://en.wikipedia.org/wiki/Mary_Louise_Smith_(civil_rights_activist)

Wikipedia. (modified) 10 Apr 2015. *Henry Gerber*.
http://en.wikipedia.org/wiki/Henry_Gerber

Wikipedia. 28 Apr 2015. *The Advocate*.
http://en.wikipedia.org/wiki/The_Advocate

Wikipedia. (modified) 30 Apr 2015. *Women's Studies*.
http://en.wikipedia.org/wiki/Women's_studies

Wikipedia. (modified) 4 May 2015 [a]. *Bayard Rustin*.
http://en.wikipedia.org/wiki/Bayard_Rustin

Wikipedia. (modified) 4 May 2015 [b]. *States With Same-Sex Marriage in the
United States*. http://en.wikipedia.org/wiki/Same-
sex_marriage_in_the_United_States

Williams, Donnie & Wayne Greenhaw. 2005. *The Thunder of Angels: The
Montgomery Bus Boycott and the People Who Broke the Back of Jim Crow*. Chicago:
Chicago University Press.

Williams, Marco. 2006. *Ten Days that Unexpectedly Changed America: Freedom
Summer*. History Channel

Willis, John C. (accessed) 3 May 2015/1 Jan 1831.*The Liberator Inaugural
Editorial by William Lloyd Garrison* (Reprinted from Wendell Phillips Garrison.
1885. *William Lloyd Garrison, 1805-1879: The Story of His Life, Told by His
Children*. Vol 1:pp224-226. (New York: The Century Company)
http://static.sewanee.edu/faculty/Willis/Civil_War/documents/Liberator.ht
ml

Wilson, William Julius. 1987. *The Truly Disadvantaged*. Chicago: University of
Chicago Press. 1987.

Wilson, William Julius. 1996. *When Work Disappears*. New York: Random House Vintage.

Wise, Tim. 2005. *White Like Me: Reflection on Race from a Privileged Son*. New York: Soft Skull Press. P.153

WOAR (Women Organized Against Rape). 2014. *Sampling of WOAR's Accomplishments Over the Past 40 Years*. Philadelphia: Women Organized Against Rape. http://www.woar.org/docs/SAMPLINGOFWOARACCOMPLISHMENTS .pdf

WOAR (Women Organized Against Rape). 2015. *About WOAR: Bringing Communities Together to End Sexual Violence*. http://www.woar.org/about-woar.php

Wolfson, Evan. 2005. *Why Marriage Matters: America, Equality, and Gay People's Right to Marry*. New York: Simon & Schuster

Wormser, Richard. 2002 [a]. *The Rise and Fall of Jim Crow: Jim Crow Stories: National Association of Colored Women*. Educational Broadcasting Corporation. http://www.pbs.org/wnet/jimcrow/stories_org_nacw.html

Wormser, Richard. 2002 [b]. *The Rise and Fall of Jim Crow: Jim Crow Stories: Morgan v. Virginia (1946)*. Educational Broadcasting Corporation. http://www.pbs.org/wnet/jimcrow/stories_events_morgan.html

X, Malcolm & Haley, Alex. 1964/1999. *The Autobiography of Malcolm X: As Told to Alex Haley*. New York: Ballantine Books.

Zald, Mayer N. & John D. McCarthy. 1979. *The Dynamics of Social Movements: Resource Mobilization, Social Control, and Tactics*. Cambridge, MA: Winthrop.

Zinn, Howard. 1964. *SNCC: The New Abolitionists*. Boston: Beacon Press.

Zinn, Howard, Dana Frank, & Robin D.G. Kelley. 2001. *Three Strikes: Miners, Musician, Salesgirls, and the Fighting Spirit of Labor's Last Century*. Boston: Beacon Press.

Endnotes

1 Declaration of Independence, and First Amendment to the Constitution of the United States
2 Feagin 2000
3 ibid
4 Bible: Luke 18:2-5
5 Baldwin 21Dec 1963 In Wise 2005
6 Gloria Steinem 2006 In Paola di Florio
7 Wise 2005:153
8 "There is no . . . place called "justice," if by that we envision a finish line, or a point at which the battle is won and the need to continue the struggle over with" because "even when you succeed in obtaining a measure of justice, you're always forced to mobilize to defend that which you've won." (Wise 2005:153-54)
9 Wise 2005:152-53.
10 Wise 2005:155
11 Tutu In Wise 2005:153
12 Wise 2005:154
13 Tarrow 1994; Tilly 2004
14 Hoffer 1951; Canetti 1966; Schnapp 2006
15 Canetti 1966; Schnapp 2006
16 Goodwin & Jasper 2003; Kornhauser 1959
17 The mid-20th century movements here referred to include the multiple branches of the racial civil rights movement, the New Left, the anti- (Vietnam) war movement, and the various branches of U.S. feminist movement.
18 Goodwin & Jasper 2003
19 Tarrow 1994
20 Tilly 2004
21 Tarrow 1994
22 Goodwin & Jasper 2003; Blumberg 2003; Tarrow 1998; McAdam et al. 1996; McAdam 1982; Zald & McCarthy 1979
23 McAdam 1982; Tarrow 1998; Goodwin & Jasper 2003:12; Farber 1994: Jasper & Nelkin 1992; Touraine 1985/1977
24 Tarrow 1998, 1994; Goodwin & Jasper 2003; D'Emilio 2003
25 Goodwin & Jasper 2003:12
26 D'Emilio 2003; Goodwin & Jasper 2003:12
27 Goodwin & Jasper 2003:12
28 Tarrow 1994
29 Tarrow 1994
30 Goodwin & Jasper 2003:3
31 Anderson 1994:176; Tarrow 1994
32 Anderson 1994:176
33 Tilly 2004

34 ibid

35 Tilly 2004; Tarrow 1994; Goodwin & Jasper 2003

36 Goodwin & Jasper 2003:3

37 Whelehan 1995; Jamieson 1995; Gamson 2003; Warner 1999

38 First and early-second-wave feminists argued a homogeneous category of "woman" as oppressed class, suffering on grounds of gender under the sexist misogyny of patriarchy. Second-wave feminists of color critiqued the tunnel-vision of this category, for its assumption of the category of "woman" as homogeneously White and middle-class, and its corresponding failure to see the differences in the experiences of oppression for women of color and working class women along continuums of multiple, interlocking oppressions. Lorde 1983; hooks 1984/2000

39 Also an unexamined category universalized as White and middle-class

40 While the rights of men of color remained contested another century, and even today, suffragists like Sojourner Truth, nonetheless, argued for the inclusion of women of color in the category of "woman."

41 Melucci 1996; Goodwin & Jasper 2003

42 Tarrow 1994

43 Farber 1994: Jasper & Nelkin 1992; Touraine 1977; Goodwin & Jasper 2003

44 Farber 1994: 1-2

45 ibid

46 Farber 1994:3

47 Farber 1994:2

48 Farber 1994:3

49 ibid

50 Farber 1994:3

51 ibid

52 Zinn 1964; Williams. 2006.

53 Now - a part of Philadelphia. Then - just beyond the limits of the city.

54 See: First Protest Against Slavery Location: 5109 Germantown Avenue, Philadelphia, 19844. Text: "Here in 1688, at the home of Tunes Kunders, an eloquent protest was written by a group of German Quakers. Signed by Pastorius and three others, it preceded by 92 years Pennsylvania's passage of the nation's first state abolition law." Explore PAHistory.com [1st Protest]. 2011; John Greenleaf Whittier, circa 1860. ["Born to Quaker parents in Massachusetts, John Greenleaf Whittier (1807-1892) edited an abolitionist newspaper in Philadelphia in the late 1830s, then left the city after witnessing the burning of Pennsylvania Hall in 1838. By the 1840s Whittier was one of the nation's most celebrated poets and influential abolitionists. In 1872 he published "The Pennsylvania Pilgrim," a long poem on William Pastorius that brought the previously little-known story of the German Quakers' 1688 protest against slavery to a national audience.] Explore PAHistory.com [Whittier]; Whittier 1872/(accessed) 3May 2015

55 Haber 1970

56 ExplorePAhistory.com [Christiana Riot]. 2011; Anderson 2007-2015; history.com [Christiana] 2015

57 Willis (accessed) 3May 2015

58 To name a few: Frederick Douglass, Sojourner Truth, William Still, Charles Henry

Langston and John Mercer Langston

59 To name a few: Lucretia Coffin Mott, Sarah and Angelina Grimke, Elizabeth Cady Stanton, Lucy Stone, Susan B. Anthony, Thomas Garrett, William Lloyd Garrison, Wendell Phillips, John Greenleaf Whittier, Harriet Beecher Stowe

60 HistoryWiz.com (accessed) 2May 2015

61 Tarrow 1994

62 Halsall 1997

63 U.E. News. 2003

64 Zinn et al. 2001; UMWA. (accessed) 28Jan 2014); libcom.org (accessed) 28Jan 2014

65 Tony Michels. 1996/2014

66 Berger 20Feb 2011

67 AFL-Cio (accessed) 3May 2015

68 ibid

69 Along with post-war federal policies undergirding housing and education for primarily European-Americans

70 Zinn et al. 2001

71 Ehrenreicht 2001; Wilson 1996, 1987; Anderson 1999

72 Zinn et al. 2001:1

73 ibid

74 ibid

75 ibid

76 Polaris Project. 2015 [a]; Polaris Project. 2015 [b]

77 Faderman 1999; Evans 1989

78 PBS 2015. Peck 2015

79 Anthony 1887; Lawrence 2010

80 ibid

81 Stannard 1977

82 At the time, when women addressed them, mixed gender public gatherings were called "promiscuous" assemblies.

83 Stannard 1977; Anthony 1881; DuBois 1998

84 At the beginning of the first-wave, a woman did not exist, legally. Guardianship of her was transferred from father to husband at marriage. If she were heir to any property (if her father had no male heirs), it became her husband's at marriage, and he could use or dispose of it without her knowledge or consent. A woman had no right to enact contracts, sue or be sued, sit on a jury, or initiate any form of legal action in the courts. Following the British Common Law doctrine of *Coverture*, unless concurrently orphaned, adult, and unmarried, a woman was always under the "covering" of a man, and her surname indicated to which man she belonged – father or husband.

85 Rupp & Taylor 1987

86 Feagin 2001; Alba 1990; Bell & Lennon 2003; Gates et al. 2003.

87 Lipsitz 1998

88 National Archives (accessed) 3May 2015

89 Royce 1993; Harrell 2014

90 Pollard, Sam (dir.). 2012. PBS: Slavery by Another Name. Twin Cities Public

Television; see also, Blackmon, Douglas A. 2008. Slavery by Another Name: The Re-Enslavement of Black Americans form the Civil War to World War II. NY: Doubleday.

91 Painter 1996; Marcus Garvey Tribute 2014

92 Wormser 2002. "The NACW adopted the motto "Lifting as We Climb."

93 BIHE 2005; A&E/History.com 2015: With the passage of the 14th Amendment in 1868, and the 15th Amendment in 1870, African American males were supposed to have secured voting rights (Black women would not be "legally" included until the passage of the 19th Amendment in 1920, purportedly giving voting rights to women of all colors), but after Reconstruction, the passage – state by state – of Jim Crow laws imposed literacy tests and poll taxes and outright violence to deprive Black males (and after 1920, Black females as well) from their exercise of the electoral franchise. One of the primary fights of the Civil Rights Movement was for enforcement of the right of African Americans to vote, including Freedom Summer in Mississippi in 1964 – a voter's rights education and resistance project undertaken by the *Congress on Racial Equality* (CORE) and the *Student Nonviolent Coordinating Committee* (SNCC) – and the march across the Edmund Pettus Bridge in Selma, Alabama on Bloody Sunday (March 7, 1965). These direct actions – and the pricking of White Northern conscience that came about through the murders of Michael Schwerner, Andrew Goodman, James Chaney, Viola Liuzzo, and James Reeb, and Jimmie Lee Jackson, and the televised beating of Amelia Boynton and the Selma marchers – led to the political pressure that brought passage of the 1965 Voting Rights Act.

94 EJI 2014; McKay 2015; u-s-history.com. 2015; Gibson 2015; Robertson 2015: Lynching of Black victims, generally but not exclusively male, were epidemic from the end of Reconstruction until the 1950s, with lynching occurring an average of 150 times per year, across the United States, East, West, South, and North.

95 Wormser 2002

96 NAACP 2009-2015 [a]

97 NAACP 2009-2015 [b]

98 In 1942, Rustin also resisted segregation on public transportation, as did Irene Morgan (in 1946, Virginia; Wormser 2002[b]), and Sarah Louise Keys (Aug 1, 1952, North Carolina - Bell, T. Anthony. 20Feb 2014; OHM 2013; WDN 2012; Wikipedia 10Feb 2015). See also: http://en.wikipedia.org/wiki/Rosa_Parks

99 Singer et al. 2006

100 Goodwin and Jasper 2003:12; See also Blumberg 2003

101 CensusScope.org (accessed) 29Apr 2015.

102 Hampton 1986

103 Time and space – here – do not permit a full delineation of the (ongoing) African American fight for full education (including underground schools under slavery and the post-slavery freedman's schools) – or of the more time-limited fight for school integration. Important players in the fight for integration include (but are by no means limited to) the plaintiffs (students and parents) of the 1954 Brown v Board of Education suit (and the cases that led up to it); The Little Rock Nine (Ernest Green, Elizabeth Eckford, Jefferson Thomas, Terrence Roberts, Carlotta Walls LaNier, Minnijean Brown, Gloria Ray Karlmark, Thelma Mothershed, and Melba Pattillo Beals) in 1957 in Little Rock, AR; Ruby Bridges in 1960 in New Orleans, LA; and

James Meredit in 1962 in Oxford, MS at the University of Mississippi.

104 Chase 2012; iampunha 17Jan 2014
105 ibid
106 Kelley 2010
107 Chase 2012
108 Who helped more than 500 to freedom and secretary of the New York Vigilance Committee; See: Chase 2012
109 Chase. 2012
110 Also a precursor to Rosa Parks in that Parks was *Secretary* of the Montgomery, Alabama chapter of the NAACP.
111 Chase 2012
112 ibid
113 Hampton & Fayer 1990; Douglass In Chase 2012; Douglass 1855
114 Chase 2012; Chase 2006
115 Mabee in Lapham 2015 [b]
116 Lapham 2015 [b].
117 Lapham 2015 [b]; BrightMoments.com 2015
118 Lapham 2015 [b]
119 Lapham 2015 [a]; see also: Mabee 1995; Mabee In Lapham 2015 [b]
120 ibid
121 Mabee in Lapham 2015 [b]
122 Lapham 2015 [b]; Mabee 1995
123 Mabee in Lapham 2015 [b]
124 ibid
125 ibid
126 Lapham 2015 [b]; Mabee 1995
127 Mabee in Lapham 2015 [b]
128 iampunha 2014
129 ibid
130 ibid
131 ibid
132 Hampton & Fayer 1990:18; Kelley 2010
133 National Archives (accessed) 29Apr 2015
134 Hampton & Fayer 1990:18
135 DarbyHistory.com (accessed) 29Apr 2015; Temple University Library (accessed) 28Apr 2015
136 "Progressivism and self-interest sometimes go hand in hand, and obviously, there was money to be made in selling streetcar tickets to Black Philadelphians." Quote. See Transcript: HistoryMakingProductions.com 26 Apr 2011 [air date]. *Philadelphia: The Great Experiment, Episode 1 (The Floodgates Open (1865-1876).* (Minute 13:40 →17:25)
137 DarbyHistory.com (accessed) 29Apr 2015
138 In DarbyHistory.com. (accessed) 29Apr 2015 [Peace Collection, Swarthmore College].
139 "In 1859, [William] Still challenged the segregation of the city's public transit system, which had separate seating for whites and blacks. He kept lobbying and, In

1865, the Pennsylvania legislature passed a law to integrate streetcars across the state;" Still "began his campaign for the rights of colored people to ride on the cars in 1859 with an article in the *North American and United States Gazette*, asking why, in the "City of Brotherly Love," should those who are taxed to support highways be rejected from those very highways." (Quote In Darby History.com 29Apr 2015; See also: Temple University Library (accessed) 28Apr 2015)

140 HistoryMakingProductions.com 26 Apr 2011 [air date]

141 The bill that passed was "prepared by the Equal Rights League" and fought for by Still, Catto, LeCount, and some other Philadelphia abolitionists. It "forbid railway corporations to exclude or segregate black passengers" and to "carry all passengers "without preference or distinction to color,"" and was approved in the PA Senate 27 to 15. (Railroad Museum of Pennsylvania. (accessed) 30Apr 2015)

142 ibid

143 HistoryMakingProductions.com 26 Apr 2011 [air date]; DarbyHistory.com (accessed) 29Apr 2015; Railroad Museum of Pennsylvania. (accessed) 30Apr 2015.

144 Railroad Museum of Pennsylvania. (accessed) 30Apr 2015.

145 Transcript: HistoryMakingProductions.com. air date 26 Apr 2011. *Episode 1 (Minute 13:40 →17:25)*.

146 ibid

147 Wikipedia (modified) 7 Feb 2015

148 HistoryMakingProductions.com. 24 Jan 2013 [airdate]. *Episode 3*

149 ibid

150 ibid; see also Hagenmayer, S. Joseph. 3Dec 1998. *Carolyn Moore, 82, A Civil-Rights Leader*. Philadelphia Inquirer. http://articles.philly.com/1998-12-03/news/25722973_1_philadelphia-transit-naacp-civil-rights

151 Moore "led protests" that integrated the Philadelphia YWCA. Charles Blockson, of Temple University, also credits Moore with the desegregation of the movie theaters in Norristown, PA. (Hagenmayer. 3Dec 1998.)

152 Hagenmayer 3Dec 1998.

153 ibid

154 ibid

155 HistoryMakingProductions.com. 24 Jan 2013 [airdate]. *Episode 3*.

156 Irene Morgan. (accessed) 28Apr 2015. http://en.wikipedia.org/wiki/Irene_Morgan

157 Irene Morgan (Wikipedia. (modified) 15Mar 2015); Bayard Rustin (Wikipedia. (modified) 4May 2015).

158 Robinson 1987

159 ibid

160 In the same incident, a pregnant adult, Mrs. Ruth Hamilton, also refused to give up her seat, but was not arrested, as a male gave up his seat for her, and she moved back (Williams & Greenhaw 2007; Phibbs 2009)

161 Aurelia Browder (Wikipedia. (modified) 16Mar 2015 [a])

162 Mary Louise Smith. (Wikipedia. (modified) 16Mar 2015 [b])

163 Claudette Colvin (Hoose 2010); Aurelia Eliseera Shine Browder (Coleman) (Trenholm State Technical College Archives (accessed) 30Apr 2015)

164 Theoharis 2014; Thoharis, Woodard & Gore 2009; Williams & Greenhaw 2005;

Brinkley 2005; Brinkley 2000

165 Hampton & Fayer 1990:p.22

166 Robinson 1987

167 A repeat of the temporarily successful boycott of 1900 to 1902

168 Zinn 1964

169 Fanon 1991

170 See Hamilton & Carmichael 1967, Cleaver 1967; Seale 1970; Malcolm X 1964

171 Hilty 2006

172 Freeman 2004 [a]

173 SLATE Archives.org 2003-2005

174 ibid

175 Not an acronym, but meant to stand for "a slate of" political "candidates who ran on a common platform." Organized at the University of California, Berkeley in 1958. Ongoing until 1966. "Approved" by the "university administration . . . as a student organization. (Wikipedia (modified) 9Mar 2015)

176 SLATE Archives.org 2003-2005; Freeman 2004 [a], 2004 [b]; Cohen & Zelnik 2002

177 SLATE Archives.org 2003-2005

178 SLATE Archives.org 2003-2005; Kitchell 1990

179 Freeman 2004 [a], 2004 [b]; Breines 1989; Cohen & Zelnik 2002

180 Freeman 2004 [a]

181 Wells 1999

182 ibid

183 ibid

184 ibid

185 ibid

186 ibid

187 Wells 1999; Barringer 1998

188 Wells 1999

189 Barringer 1998

190 Farber 1994

191 Wells 1999

192 ibid

193 ibid

194 ibid

195 ibid

196 Barringer 1998; Farber 1994

197 Initially called by Paul, *The Lucretia Mott Amendment*

198 Freeman 1971

199 Faderman 1999 documents the lesbians/women-identified-women/romantic friends (and their relationships) at the forefront of the first-wave.

200 Lorde 1984; Stein 1997

201 Beal 1970

202 Lorde 1983

203 McIntosh 1989; Tatum 1997; Frankenberg 1993

204 hooks 1984; Combahee 1977

205 Moraga & Anzaldua 1984; Combahee 1977; Hill Collins 2000; Lorde 1983
206 Boston Women's Health Collective 1970; Evans 2006; Bloom 1995/2014
207 Brownmiller 1975; Warshaw 1988
208 WOAR 2014; WOAR 2015
209 ibid
210 Women's Studies: Wikipedia 30Apr 2015; SDSU 20Jan 2015;
National Women's History Project: NWHP 4May 2015
211 Graff 1999, Evans 1989
212 ibid
213 ibid
214 Some gay and lesbian bars were race- and class- and sexual-taste segregated.
Others were more mixed.
215 Weeks 1977, 1981, Adam 1995; Steakley 1993; Katz 1976
216 Faderman 1999; McGarry 1998
217 Silverman & Stryker 2005
218 Chauncey 2004
219 Chauncey 2004:14
220 Chauncey 2004:11
221 Chauncey 2004:18
222 Chauncey 2004:16
223 Chauncey 2004:5; Russo 1981
224 Chauncey 2004:18
225 Goodman & Maggio 2004
226 Chauncey 2004:11
227 Schiller & Rosenberg 1984
228 Chauncey 2004:11
229 Chauncey 2004:6
230 ibid
231 Chauncey 2004:21
232 Chauncey 2004:7, 18
233 Chauncey 2004:8-9, 11
234 Chauncey 2004:10
235 Rupp 1999:143
236 Chauncey 2004:9
237 Henry Gerber (PBS 2014)
238 Chauncey 2004:9, 27
239 ibid
240 Chauncey 2004:9 - The U.S. Supreme Court limited the Comstock Act in 1958.
241 Henry Gerber also drew some connections about homosexuals as an oppressed
group – Dupre 1998; Adam 1995; Rupp 1999; See also: Kepner & Murray 2002;
Rosario 2002; CGLHF 2014; Wikipedia (modified) 10 Apr 2014; PBS 2014.
242 Rupp 1999:162
243 Adam 1995:67
244 ibid
245 Adam 1995:67-8; See also Timmon 1990; Katz 1976, 412
246 Rupp 1999:163

247 D'Emilio & Freedman 1988:292; Corey 1951

248 Adam 1995:68

249 Chauncey 2004:28

250 Rupp 1999:159

251 ibid

252 Chauncey 2004:27

253 Chauncey 2004:27-28

254 Barbara Gittings: jessamyn 30 Mar 2013; Free Library of Philadelphia 2015

255 Rupp 1999:165

256 Rupp 1999:166

257 Rupp 1999:164

258 Rupp 1999:166

259 Rupp 1999:167

260 Philadelphia - Pratt 2004-2006 (glbtq inc.)

261 Rupp 1999:167-68

262 The Advocate - Wikipedia 28 Apr 2015

263 Goodwin & Jasper 2003:12-13; D'Emilio 2003

264 Goodwin & Jasper 1003:13

265 So named because the site of the initial rioting, the Stonewall Inn, is located in New York's Greenwich Village at 43 *Christopher Street*.

266 Rupp 1999:177

267 D'Emilio 2003:34

268 In journalistic venues like the *Village Voice* and *Harper's*

269 D'Emilio 2003:34

270 Chauncey 2004: 31-32

271 First Gay Pride March - Sargeant 2010

272 Rupp 1999:177

273 Gay Liberation Front - Bateman 2004 [a]

274 Gay Activist Alliance - IGIC 4 May 2015

275 Chauncey 2004:39

276 Chauncey 2004:31

277 2013 – Consensual adult-to-adult anal (and sometimes oral) intercourse (classed as sodomy) was a felony in all 50 states until 1962, and was still a felony in 49 states in 1976. In 2003, sodomy remained a felony in 17 states. Despite the 2003 U.S. Supreme Court Lawrence v. Texas ruling that declared all sodomy statutes in the U.S. unconstitutional, 14 states (unconstitutionally) maintain sodomy laws on their books: Alabama, Florida, Idaho, Kansas, Louisiana, Michigan, Missouri, Mississippi, North Carolina, Oklahoma, South Carolina, Utah, Virginia and Texas. (Equality Matters 2011); The state sodomy laws still on the books in Kansas, Missouri, Oklahoma, and Texas only apply to same-sex partners. (Ring 17 Apr 2013); "[D]espite the fact that the Lawrence v. Texas decision renders these laws unconstitutional," "LGBT[Q] people in Michigan "are still at risk of spending 15 years in state prison for acts that are perfectly legal in most other states [and constitutionally legal according to the U.S. Supreme Court]." Further, "someone convicted under Michigan's [unconstitutional] *Abominable and Detestable Crime Against Nature statute*, and a separate "*Gross Indecency*" law, must register with the state as sex offenders. They "continue to be charged with

crimes for public speech, in which they let another person know they are interested in private, unpaid sex with another adult," and are entrapped by "Bag-A-Fag (undercover decoy cop) operations, where police officers pretend to be gay men cruising for unpaid, consensual sex. . . . [P]rosecutors in some states, especially Louisiana, have used sodomy laws to push for harsher penalties against LGBT[Q] suspects than they would for heterosexual suspects accused of engaging in the exact same behavior, such as prostitution or public sex . . . . Activists say . . . transgender women and young gay men who have been rejected by their families for being gay or transgender [sometimes] engage in prostitution as a means of survival . . . [and] members of these two groups have been among those most frequently charged under [these unconstitutional sodomy statutes] . . . . "Even though the laws are clearly unconstitutional, their existence in the legal code gives officers the cover they need to arrest and prosecute gay people," he said. "Sometimes officers simply choose to ignore Lawrence altogether in an attempt to enforce state sodomy laws as if the decision never occurred."" (Chibbaro Jr. 17 Apr 2013)

278 Lambda Legal 4 May 2015
279 National LGBTQ Task Force 4 May 2015
280 ibid
281 HRC.org 4 May 2015
282 http://www.glaad.org/about/history.php
283 Chauncey 2004:28
284 Chauncey 2004:34
284 ibid
285 ibid
286 ibid
287 ibid
288 Chauncey 2004:35
289 Chauncey 2004:38-39
290 ibid
291 At the end of her life, Tammy Faye (Bakker) Messner came out as strongly pro-gay.
292 Chauncey 2004:39-40
293 Chauncey 2004:41
294 ibid
295 Bateman 2004 [b]
296 ibid; see also Chauncey 2004:41
297 Chambre 2006
298 Kaczorowski 2002
299 ibid
300 ibid
301 ibid
302 Perry 2006; private conversations
303 Kaczorowski 2002
304 ibid
305 Inness 2002
306 Bronski 2003 [a]

307 Forrest 2005
308 Bronski 2003 [a]
309 Scagliotti 2003
310 D'Emilio 2003:34
311 Chauncey 2004: 33
312 ibid
313 D'Emilio 2003:34
314 D'Emilio 2003:34-35
315 ibid
316 Chauncey 2004:34-35
317 Stacey 1990; Coontz 1998
318 Coontz 2000
319 Chauncey 2004:59
320 ibid
321 Sullivan-Blum 2003:159-60
322 Blum 2001
323 Gay Marriage Bureau Takeover 1971 (Uploaded on Mar 15, 2010.
http://www.youtube.com/watch?v=Z7NU8B1EGnU ("The Gay Activist Alliance
decided to occupy NYC's Marriage License Bureau, June 4,1971, after the City Clerk
threatened to arrest the minister of a local gay church for performing "Services of
Holy Union" which the City Clerk said were the equivalent of gay marriage. Gay
marriage was not yet one of the LGBT movement's goal in 1971 but the activists felt
they couldn't stand by while a city official threatened the Church of the Beloved
Disciple with legal action. They decided to take over the NYC Marriage License
Bureau and throw an engagement party for two gay couples. Here, they plan their
action in the GAA Firehouse headquarters on Wooster Street in NYC and begin their
invasion.")
324 Chauncey 2004
325 Goldstein 2006: That "marriage is the only nomenclature" that will secure all of
"the rights we want."; See also: Wolfson 2005; Kotulski 2004
326 BeyondMarriage.org 26 Jul 2006
327 Chauncey 2004; Stacey 1990; Coontz 2005; See also: D'Emilio & Freedman 1988;
Hartog 2000; Cott 2000
328 Sullivan-Blum 2003:161.
329 Boswell 1995:38
330 ibid
331 Boswell 1995
332 D'Emilio & Freeman 1988; Coontz 2005; Graff 2005; Schneider 1980; Rubin
1984; Gordis 1993; Shapiro 1984
333 Shapiro 1984:18
334 Graff 2005
335 Rubin 1975; Leacock 1978; Blackwood 1999
336 Levi-Strauss 1969; Shapiro 1984; Rubin 1975:174
337 Silverblatt 1987; Stoler 1989; Stolcke 1993; McClintock 1995
338 Sullivan-Blum 2003
339 Boswell 1994:29

340 ibid

341 Adam 1995; Graff 1999; Boswell 1994; Coontz 2005

342 Boswell 1995:32

343 Boswell 1995:xxi

344 Graff 2005

345 Adam 1995

346 Graff 2005

347 Gies and Gies 1987:55

348 In the discussion of arranged marriage, men are always considered to have been good with – or capable of engaging and performing sexually with – whomever they were required to marry; and yet, even today (in many cultures) men are pressured to marry at times when, or to partners who, they would not have so chosen. Nevertheless, it is evident that if a man were not turned on (not aroused) by (or was even turned off by) the spouse he was required to achieve penetration with, he might experience more functional difficulty than the woman who has(had) ("only") to submit (rape or rape-like as that was/is), but not perform (at least, not until childbirth). It is rational to suspect that it might be difficult as a man to force intercourse upon a girl/woman who is repulsed by or frightened of or rejecting of you. It might also be difficult to engage in intercourse with a girl/woman who (for one of a myriad of reasons) repulses you. And further still, there is evidence in some of the history of arranged marriages (for instance, among royalty or the nobility), that some bridegrooms may have been so same-sex oriented (predominantly gay/ or more homosexual than bisexual) that their ability to create a male heir – with the (female) partner to which they were involuntarily assigned – was compromised.

349 Boswell 1995; Chauncey 2004; Van Grubbs 1994

350 Chauncey 2004:61

351 Ennen 1989

352 Knight 2010; SCBorromeo.org. (accessed) 4 May 2015

353 Chauncey 2004:59

354 Boswell 1995:xxi

355 Boswell 1995:xx

356 Graff 2005

357 ibid

358 Halsall 1996; Ennen 1989:105

359 Waterworth 1848

360 Graff 2005

361 D'Emilio & Freedman 1988: xi-xii

362 Coontz 2005

363 Graff 1999:xiii

364 Graff 1999:xiii; D'Emilio & Freedman 1988:xi

365 Graff 1999:xiii

366 Chauncey 2004:59

367 Graff 2005

368 D'Emilio & Freedman 1988:xi-xii, xv

369 Gazit 2003

370 D'Emilio & Freedman 1988: xvi

371 Graff 1999:xiii
372 Chauncey 2004:59
373 Graff 1999:xiii
374 Chauncey 2004: 59
375 Chauncey 2004:61-2
376 Chauncey 2004:61; Cott 2000:47-52
377 Chauncey 2004:60-1, 65
378 Chauncey 2004:61
379 Chauncey 2004:60
380 ibid
381 Shapiro 1984; Amadiume 1987; Hinsch 1990; Gordis 1993; Hendrix 1997;
Sullivan-Blum 2003; Murray 2000
382 Sullivan-Blum 2003:159-60
383 Sullivan-Blum 2003:159-60; See also Shapiro 1984; Amadiume 1987; Murray
2000
384 See also Evans-Pritchard 1970,; van Onselen 1984; Murray 2000
385 See also Murray 2000; Hinsch 1990; Shapiro 1984; Blackwood 1984; Hendrix
1997
386 Sullivan-Blum 2003:161
387 Sullivan-Blum 2003:160
388 Murray 2000; Goulet 1996; Thomas & Jacobs 1999
389 Adam 1995; Chauncey 2004
390 Demian 2015
391 Adam 1995
392 Faderman 1981; Adam 1995
393 D'Emilio and Freedman 1988:xx
394 Graff 1999:xiv
395 ibid
396 Graff 1999: xiii-xiv; Pharr 1997
397 Graff 1999:xiv
398 e.g. Jerry Falwell's Moral Majority in 1979; Family Protection Act (D'Emilio and
Freedman 1988:350)
399 D'Emilio and Freedman 1988:348
400 Graff 2005
401 Boswell 1995
402 Boswell 1995:xxii
403 FreedomtoMarry.org. 2003-2015; Margolin 14 Feb 2014; The 1996 Defense of
Marriage Act (DOMA), for the first time ever and only in regard to this one issue,
allowed one state to refuse to recognize another states laws – to violate the *unitedness*
of the "United" States, by not engaging in Full Faith and Credit between states. It
allows a state to not recognize the marriages of same-sex couples – to refuse to
recognize the valid same-sex marriages of couples enacted in a state that does grant
them legal civil marriage. Also, through DOMA, the federal government refused
recognition to all same-sex couples married within any state. Denial of access to
federal recognition (of their legal state marriages) disallowed same-sex couples access
to over 1,100 protections and responsibilities that automatically attach to other-sex

marriage. A majority of states (31 at this writing) still prohibit same-sex couples from marrying through either their own state-level legislative DOMAs, or because they amended their state constitutions (since 1993) to prohibit same-sex marriages. On 26 Jun 2013, the U.S. Supreme Court in their *Windsor v. United States* decision struck down Section 3 of the federal-level DOMA (which dealt with federal recognition of same-sex unions), granting federal recognition to couples legally married within any state – thus allowing those couples to, among other things, file their federal income taxes jointly and to receive spousal social security benefits upon the death of their spouse. The U.S. Supreme Court failed to strike down sections 1 and 2 of DOMA, thus, still allowing states to NOT recognize valid same-sex marriages from other states. Thus, the fight goes on, with the political Right now filing new legislation to reinstitute the federal ban (the part of DOMA that was struck down) on recognition of same-sex unions.

404 Boswell 1995:xxii

405 MCC 2013 [a]; MCC 2013 [b]; MCC 2015

406 Perry 2006 [b]; At about the same time, civil rights activist and United Methodist minister Cecil Williams also began to officiate over "same-sex blessings." (Kotulski 2004:70)

407 Warner 2002

408 ibid

409 ibid

410 MCC 2013 [b]

411 Perry 2006 [a]

412 MCC 2013 [b]

413 "On May 15, 2008, in a historic victory, the California Supreme Court ruled in favor of Rev. Troy Perry, his husband Phillip Ray De Blieck, and fellow litigants, making same-gender marriage legal in California. The court rules that the state constitution guarantees same-sex couples the right to marry." (MCC 2013 [b])

414 Stacey 2002

415 ibid

416 Twenty years after the initial 1993 state Supreme Court ruling, in 2013, the Hawaiian legislature passed, and the governor signed into law, a bill making same-sex marriage legal in that state. Same-sex couples became able to marry in Hawaii on December 2, 2013. (Gonzalez 2 Dec 2013)

417 Stacey 2002:397-98; Johnson 2015; Bérubé 1990 - On November 30th, 1993, Clinton announced "Don't Ask, Don't Tell" – an anti-gay policy initially touted as better than the previous policy of the military to Ask (or to, essentially, witch-hunt)– and then issue discharges (administrative, undesirable, Regulation 615-360, Section 8 ["mentally unfit"], or dishonorable) – which then shamed those discharged and generally disallowed the discharged access to veteran's benefits. Under *Don't Ask, Don't Tell*, over 12,500 service personnel were discharged. This policy was overturned September 20th, 2011.

418 Such an amendment would have prevented states, or the U.S. Supreme Court, from legalizing same-sex marriage and overridden the 2004 Massachusetts law (and subsequent state laws) recognizing same-sex marriage.

419 This ruling, and subsequent legal compliance with this ruling, were contested by

conservatives. Early on, it looked likely that they would, like Hawai'i, lose marriage again, but the opponents of same-sex marriage were unsuccessful in amending that state's constitution and same-sex marriages have been unmolested in Massachusetts since they began.

420 Internationally, Denmark became the first nation to legalize same-sex civil unions in 1989. The Netherlands became the first to legalize same-sex marriage in 2001, followed by Belgium in 2003, and Canada, Spain, and South Africa in 2005 (with the South African Parliament complying legislatively on November 15, 2006), while many countries increasingly recognize civil unions and domestic partnerships of varying kinds; including: Andorra, Argentina, Brazil, Croatia, Czech Republic, Finland, France (1999), Germany (2001), Greenland (1996), Iceland (1996), Israel, Luxembourg, Mexico, New Zealand, Norway (1993), Portugal, Scandanavia, Slovenia, Sweden (1995), Switzerland (2000), Tasmania, and the United Kingdom (2005).

421 On October 18, 2013, the NJ State Supreme Court denied the governor's request for a stay pending appeal in regard to the trial court decision in *Garden State Equality v. Dow*, and on October 21, 2013 the *Garden State Equality v. Dow* ruling went into effect, the governor withdrew his appeal, and same-sex couple began marrying (not just 'civilly uniting') in New Jersey.

422 "The United States Supreme Court has agreed to decide whether a state may refuse to license same-sex marriages or to recognize same-sex marriages from other jurisdictions. It has heard oral arguments on April 28, 2015. A decision is expected in June." States with marriage as of May 2015: AK, AZ, CA, CO, CT, DE, FL, HI, ID, IL, IN,IA, KS, ME, MD, MA,MN, MO, MT, NV, NH,NJ, NM, NY, NC, OK, OR, PA, RI, SC, UT, VT,VA, WA, WV, WI, WY, Washington DC, and 22 Native American/First Nations tribes. (Wikipedia 4 May 2015 [b])

423 Lucy Stone. January 1852

424 and males for labor

425 Perry-Wood 2010 - 1/3rd of teen suicides are connected to sexual orientation or gender identity

426 Goodreads 2015

Made in the USA
Middletown, DE
25 January 2017